Space and Astronomy Experiments

FACTS ON FILE SCIENCE EXPERIMENTS

Space and Astronomy Experiments

Pamela Walker
Elaine Wood

Facts On File
An imprint of Infobase Publishing

Space and Astronomy Experiments

Text and artwork copyright © 2010 by Infobase Publishing

Editor: Frank K. Darmstadt
Copy Editor for A Good Thing, Inc.: Betsy Feist
Project Coordination: Aaron Richman
Art Director: Howard Petlack
Production: Victoria Kessler
Illustrations: Hadel Studios

Facts On File, Inc.
An imprint of Infobase Publishing
132 West 31st Street
New York NY 10001

Library of Congress Cataloging-in-Publication Data
Walker, Pamela.
Space and astronomy experiments / Pamela Walker, Elaine Wood.
p. cm.—(Space and astronomy experiments)
Includes bibliographical references and index.
ISBN 978-0-8160-7809-7
1. Space astronomy–Experiments–Popular works. 2. Astronomy–Experiments–Popular works. I. Wood, Elaine, 1950- II. Title.
QB136.W35 2009
500.5078–dc22 2009032825

Printed in the United States of America

Bang AGT 10 9 8 7 6 5 4 3 2

This book is printed on acid-free paper.

Contents

Preface

For centuries, humans have studied and explored the natural world around them. The ever-growing body of knowledge resulting from these efforts is science. Information gained through science is passed from one generation to the next through an array of educational programs. One of the primary goals of every science education program is to help young people develop critical-thinking and problem-solving skills that they can use throughout their lives.

Science education is unique in academics in that it not only conveys facts and skills; it also cultivates curiosity and creativity. For this reason, science is an active process that cannot be fully conveyed by passive teaching techniques. The question for educators has always been, "What is the best way to teach science?" There is no simple answer to this question, but studies in education provide useful insights.

Research indicates that students need to be actively involved in science, learning it through experience. Science students are encouraged to go far beyond the textbook and to ask questions, consider novel ideas, form their own predictions, develop experiments or procedures, collect information, record results, analyze findings, and use a variety of resources to expand knowledge. In other words, students cannot just hear science; they must also do science.

"Doing" science means performing experiments. In the science curriculum, experiments play a number of educational roles. In some cases, hands-on activities serve as hooks to engage students and introduce new topics. For example, a discrepant event used as an introductory experiment encourages questions and inspires students to seek the answers behind their findings. Classroom investigations can also help expand information that was previously introduced or cement new knowledge. According to neuroscience, experiments and other types of hands-on learning help transfer new learning from short-term into long-term memory.

Facts On File Science Experiments is a six-volume set of experiments that helps engage students and enable them to "do" science. The high-interest experiments in these books put students' minds into gear and give them opportunities to become involved, to think independently, and to build on their own base of science knowledge.

As a resource, Facts On File Science Experiments provides teachers with new and innovative classroom investigations that are presented in a clear, easy-to-understand style. The areas of study in the six-volume set include forensic science, environmental science, computer research, physical science, weather and climate, and space and astronomy. Experiments are supported by colorful figures and line illustrations that help hold students' attention and explain information. All of the experiments in these books use multiple science process skills such as observing, measuring, classifying, analyzing, and predicting. In addition, some of the experiments require students to practice inquiry science by setting up and carrying out their own open-ended experiments.

Each volume of the set contains 20 new experiments as well as extensive safety guidelines, glossary, correlation to the National Science Education Standards, scope and sequence, and an annotated list of Internet resources. An introduction that presents background information begins each investigation to provide an overview of the topic. Every experiment also includes relevant specific safety tips along with materials list, procedure, analysis questions, explanation of the experiment, connections to real life, and an annotated further reading section for extended research.

Pam Walker and Elaine Wood, the authors of Facts On File Science Experiments, are sensitive to the needs of both science teachers and students. The writing team has more than 40 years of combined science teaching experience. Both are actively involved in planning and improving science curricula in their home state, Georgia, where Pam was the 2007 Teacher of the Year. Walker and Wood are master teachers who hold specialist degrees in science and science education. They are the authors of dozens of books for middle and high school science teachers and students.

Facts On File Science Experiments, by Walker and Wood, facilitates science instruction by making it easy for teachers to incorporate experimentation. During experiments, students reap benefits that are not available in other types of instruction. One of these benefits is the opportunity to take advantage of the learning provided by social interactions. Experiments are usually carried out in small groups, enabling students to brainstorm and learn from each other. The validity of group work as an effective learning tool is supported by research in neuroscience, which shows that the brain is a social organ and that communication and collaboration are activities that naturally enhance learning.

Experimentation addresses many different types of learning, including lateral thinking, multiple intelligences, and constructivism. In lateral thinking, students solve problems using nontraditional methods. Long-established, rigid procedures for problem-solving are replaced by original ideas from students. When encouraged to think laterally, students are more likely to come up with unique ideas that are not usually found in the traditional classroom. This type of thinking requires students to construct meaning from an activity and to think like scientists.

Another benefit of experimentation is that it accommodates students' multiple intelligences. According to the theory of multiple intelligences, students possess many different aptitudes, but in varying degrees. Some of these forms of intelligence include linguistic, musical, logical-mathematical, spatial, kinesthetic, intrapersonal, and interpersonal. Learning is more likely to be acquired and retained when more than one sense is involved. During an experiment, students of all intellectual types find roles in which they can excel.

Students in the science classroom become involved in active learning, constructing new ideas based on their current knowledge and their experimental findings. The constructivist theory of learning encourages students to discover principles for and by themselves. Through problem solving and independent thinking, students build on what they know, moving forward in a manner that makes learning real and lasting.

Active, experimental learning makes connections between newly acquired information and the real world, a world that includes jobs. In the 21st century, employers expect their employees to identify and solve problems for themselves. Therefore, today's students, workers of the near future, will be required to use higher-level thinking skills. Experience with science experiments provides potential workers with the ability and confidence to be problem solvers.

The goal of Walker and Wood in Facts On File Science Experiments is to provide experiments that hook and hold the interest of students, teach basic concepts of science, and help students develop their critical-thinking skills. When fully immersed in an experiment, students can experience those "Aha!" moments, the special times when new information merges with what is already known and understanding breaks through. On these occasions, real and lasting learning takes place. The authors hope that this set of books helps bring more "Aha" moments into every science class.

Acknowledgments

This book would not exist were it not for our editor, Frank K. Darmstadt, who conceived and directed the project. Frank supervised the material closely, editing and making invaluable comments along the way. Betsy Feist of A Good Thing, Inc., is responsible for transforming our raw material into a polished and grammatically correct manuscript that makes us proud.

Introduction

The sky is, and always has been, a fascinating place for inquisitive minds. Whether wishing on a star or watching a meteor shower, almost every student has been awed by the magnitude of space. This natural fascination with space helps capture students' interest in the science of astronomy, the study of heavenly bodies, their behavior, and characteristics. As the oldest natural science, knowledge of astronomy has come from some of the world's earliest and greatest scientists, including Copernicus, Galileo, Kepler, Newton, and Einstein. By studying historically important experiments in astronomy, students gain insight into basic scientific principles and learn how early thinkers approached problem solving with little or no scientific equipment.

Modern astronomy relies on technology that has been developed in the last few decades. Current research in astronomy has made it possible for men and women to travel to the Moon, construct a space station, and send exploratory probes to other planets. Today's astronomers have also developed satellites and telescopes that collect and interpret radiation from all parts of the electromagnetic spectrum.

Space and Astronomy Experiments is one volume of the new Facts On File Science Experiments set. The goal of this volume is to provide science teachers with 20 fresh, original experiments that convey basic principles of space science and astronomy. *Space and Astronomy Experiments* includes activities that draw from historically important investigations as well as those that examine new technology. Because astronomy is an integrated science that incorporates physics, geology, Earth science, and mathematics, this book presents experiments from all areas. Each experiment in the book is a proven classroom activity that helps broaden understandings of both scientific facts and the nature of science. Appropriate for both middle and high school classes, the investigations are enjoyable and appealing.

The nature of light and the electromagnetic spectrum are examined in several experiments, including "A Simple Spectroscope to Identify Gases," in which students used a spectroscope to analyze the radiation given off by known and unknown gases. "Visible and Infrared Light" is an inquiry experiment in which students find the similarities and differences in infrared energy and visible light energy. In "Speed of Electromagnetic Energy," students work as a class to develop a scale model of the solar system, then calculate the time it takes energy from the Sun to travel to each planet. "How Does Light Intensity Vary With Distance?" provides students an opportunity to develop their own procedures and carry out their experiments. "Flashlight Magnitude" helps students understand how the scale of star brightness was established. Students learn more about the Sun and its characteristics in "Coronal Ejections," an investigation using photographs of the Sun's surface and measurements of gas ejections. "Sunspot Monitor" has students track sunspots and graph their movement over time.

Planets and their characteristics are the topics of three experiments. In "Saturn's Rings," students make a model that shows the planet's rings to scale. Students build a telescope and use it to examine Jupiter and its moons in "Viewing Jupiter Through a Simple Telescope." Characteristics of the planet Earth are studied in "How Long Is Twilight?" This investigation has students collect their own data and compare it to data collected by experts.

Student-developed investigations are an important part of *Space and Astronomy Experiments*. By performing inquiry experiments, students gain confidence in their abilities to solve problems and gain insight into the true nature of science. "How Efficient Is a Solar Panel?" is an inquiry-style experiment in which students compare energy input to the energy output of a photovoltaic cell to determine its effectiveness. In "Who Knows Ten Constellations?" students develop, conduct, and interpret a survey to find out how familiar their peers are with common constellations. "The Size of the Universe" gives students the chance to develop their own scale showing the relative distances between the Earth and distant space objects, such as stars and other galaxies.

Experiments with detailed instructions help students learn specific concepts as well as the skills needed in every science classroom. To understand some of the physics of astronomy, students can carry out "Acceleration Due to Gravity" and "The Law of Inertia." Both these experiments have students repeat techniques used by early astronomers in their quest to understand the motion of heavenly bodies. In "Kinetic Energy of Impact," students analyze the factors that affect the size of a crater and calculate the velocity of balls used to model meteorite impact.

Two experiments use model rockets to study space flight. In "Rocket Science," students assemble a model rocket and use it to find out how the payload affects duration of flight. "Measuring the Altitude and Speed of a Model Rocket" has students take measurements while their model rocket is in flight so they can calculate the height of its flight and its velocity.

If students are not absorbed in an activity, no learning takes place, so the authors have worked to make the experiments in *Space and Astronomy Experiments* fun and engaging. Our goals for this book are to offer students a chance to stretch their brains while expanding their interests in and knowledge of space and the science of astronomy.

Safety Precautions

REVIEW BEFORE STARTING ANY EXPERIMENT

Each experiment includes special safety precautions that are relevant to that particular project. These do not include all the basic safety precautions that are necessary whenever you are working on a scientific experiment. For this reason, it is absolutely necessary that you read and remain mindful of the General Safety Precautions that follow. Experimental science can be dangerous and good laboratory procedure always includes following basic safety rules. Things can happen quickly while you are performing an experiment—for example, materials can spill, break, or even catch on fire. There will not be time after the fact to protect yourself. Always prepare for unexpected dangers by following the basic safety guidelines during the entire experiment, whether or not something seems dangerous to you at a given moment.

We have been quite sparing in prescribing safety precautions for the individual experiments. For one reason, we want you to take very seriously the safety precautions that are printed in this book. If you see it written here, you can be sure that it is here because it is absolutely critical.

Read the safety precautions here and at the beginning of each experiment before performing each lab activity. It is difficult to remember a long set of general rules. By rereading these general precautions every time you set up an experiment, you will be reminding yourself that lab safety is critically important. In addition, use your good judgment and pay close attention when performing potentially dangerous procedures. Just because the book does not say "Be careful with hot liquids" or "Don't cut yourself with a knife" does not mean that you can be careless when boiling water or using a knife to punch holes in plastic bottles. Notes in the text are special precautions to which you must pay special attention.

GENERAL SAFETY PRECAUTIONS

Accidents can be caused by carelessness, haste, or insufficient knowledge. By practicing safety procedures and being alert while conducting experiments, you can avoid taking an unnecessary risk. Be sure to check the individual experiments in this book for additional safety regulations and adult supervision requirements. If you will be working in a laboratory, do not work alone. When you are working off site, keep in groups with a minimum of three students per group, and follow school rules and state legal requirements for the number of supervisors required. Ask an adult supervisor with basic training in first aid to carry a small first-aid kit. Make sure everyone knows where this person will be during the experiment.

PREPARING

- Clear all surfaces before beginning experiments.
- Read the entire experiment before you start.
- Know the hazards of the experiments and anticipate dangers.

PROTECTING YOURSELF

- Follow the directions step by step.
- Perform only one experiment at a time.
- Locate exits, fire blanket and extinguisher, master gas and electricity shut-offs, eyewash, and first-aid kit.
- Make sure there is adequate ventilation.
- Do not participate in horseplay.
- Do not wear open-toed shoes.
- Keep floor and workspace neat, clean, and dry.
- Clean up spills immediately.
- If glassware breaks, do not clean it up by yourself; ask for teacher assistance.
- Tie back long hair.
- Never eat, drink, or smoke in the laboratory or workspace.
- Do not eat or drink any substances tested unless expressly permitted to do so by a knowledgeable adult.

USING EQUIPMENT WITH CARE

- Set up apparatus far from the edge of the desk.
- Use knives or other sharp, pointed instruments with care.

- Pull plugs, not cords, when removing electrical plugs.
- Clean glassware before and after use.
- Check glassware for scratches, cracks, and sharp edges.
- Let your teacher know about broken glassware immediately.
- Do not use reflected sunlight to illuminate your microscope.
- Do not touch metal conductors.
- Take care when working with any form of electricity.
- Use alcohol-filled thermometers, not mercury-filled thermometers.

USING CHEMICALS

- Never taste or inhale chemicals.
- Label all bottles and apparatus containing chemicals.
- Read labels carefully.
- Avoid chemical contact with skin and eyes (wear safety glasses or goggles, lab apron, and gloves).
- Do not touch chemical solutions.
- Wash hands before and after using solutions.
- Wipe up spills thoroughly.

HEATING SUBSTANCES

- Wear safety glasses or goggles, apron, and gloves when heating materials.
- Keep your face away from test tubes and beakers.
- When heating substances in a test tube, avoid pointing the top of the test tube toward other people.
- Use test tubes, beakers, and other glassware made of Pyrex™ glass.
- Never leave apparatus unattended.
- Use safety tongs and heat-resistant gloves.
- If your laboratory does not have heatproof workbenches, put your Bunsen burner on a heatproof mat before lighting it.
- Take care when lighting your Bunsen burner; light it with the airhole closed and use a Bunsen burner lighter rather than wooden matches.

- Turn off hot plates, Bunsen burners, and gas when you are done.
- Keep flammable substances away from flames and other sources of heat.
- Have a fire extinguisher on hand.

FINISHING UP

- Thoroughly clean your work area and any glassware used.
- Wash your hands.
- Be careful not to return chemicals or contaminated reagents to the wrong containers.
- Do not dispose of materials in the sink unless instructed to do so.
- Clean up all residues and put in proper containers for disposal.
- Dispose of all chemicals according to all local, state, and federal laws.

BE SAFETY CONSCIOUS AT ALL TIMES!

1. Visible and Infrared Light

Topic

Energy in the visible light spectrum differs from that in the infrared spectrum.

Introduction

Energy travels as waves in the form of *electromagnetic radiation*. Radio waves, microwaves, infrared radiation, visible light, ultraviolet radiation, X-rays, and gamma rays are all forms of electromagnetic radiation. For analysis, types of electromagnetic radiation are organized into an *electromagnetic spectrum* according to the amount of energy they contain (Figure 1). On the spectrum, you can see that waves transmitting a lot of energy have shorter wavelengths and higher frequencies than waves transmitting smaller amounts of energy.

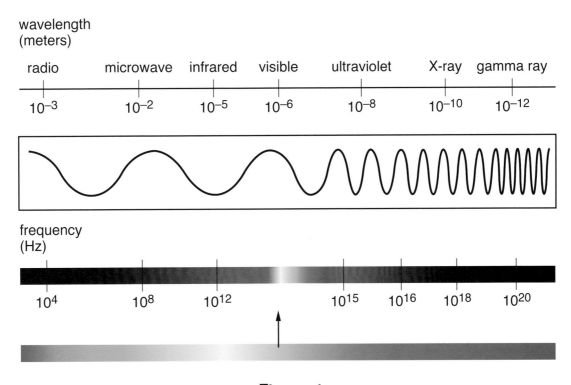

Figure 1

Electromagnetic spectrum

The electromagnetic spectrum contains a broad range of waves that have different characteristics. Radio waves can transmit a signal from your favorite radio station to your car, microwaves can pop a bag of popcorn, and X-rays can be used to view your bones. A very narrow range of electromagnetic waves make up the visible spectrum, which includes all of the colors that we can see. The Sun gives off ultraviolet radiation, visible light, and infrared radiation. In this experiment, you will use filters to isolate visible and infrared radiation and compare their characteristics. (Ultraviolet radiation will not be tested because it can be very harmful to your eyes and skin.)

Time Required

60 minutes

Materials

- incandescent lightbulb
- electric lightbulb socket
- paper towel tube
- visible light filter (allows only infrared light to pass)
- infrared light filter (allows only visible light to pass)
- 2 thermometers
- digital light meter
- prism
- access to the Internet or to books on astronomy
- science notebook

Safety Note   Use caution when working with electricity. Never look directly into infrared light. Please review and follow the safety guidelines at the beginning of this volume.

Procedure

1. Your job is to design and perform an experiment to find how visible light and infrared light differ and how they are similar.

2. You can use any of the supplies provided by your teacher, but you will not need to use all of them.

3. Before you conduct your experiment, decide exactly what you are going to do. Write the steps you plan to take (your experimental procedure) and the materials you plan to use (materials list) on the data table. Show your procedure and materials list to the teacher. If you get teacher approval, proceed with your experiment. If not, modify your work and show it to your teacher again.

4. Once you have teacher approval, assemble the materials you need and begin your procedure.

5. Collect your results on a data table of your own design.

Data Table	
Your experimental procedure	
Your materials list	
Teacher's approval	

Analysis

1. Use your textbook or the Internet to research the electromagnetic wave spectra. What are the frequency and wavelength ranges for visible and infrared light?

2. How is the wavelength of an electromagnetic wave related to its frequency and the energy that it carries?

3. Which type of electromagnetic radiation within the spectrum carries the most energy?

4. Describe how light filters are capable of isolating certain types of light.

5. How is the behavior of infrared waves different from that of visible light? Include information on heat production, visibility, and any other characteristics that were observed in this experiment.

6. List some ways that infrared light is used in everyday life. Which characteristics of these types of waves are important when it comes to their common functions?

What's Going On?

The characteristics of any type of electromagnetic energy are determined by its wavelength and frequency. Waves that have a short wavelength and high frequency carry more energy than those with a long wavelength and a low frequency. The amount of energy carried by a wave determines how that wave behaves. For instance, ultraviolet radiation is capable of causing damage to the skin because it penetrates into the skin cells. However, X-rays, which carry more energy than ultraviolet waves, are capable of penetrating through the skin and muscles. As a result, we can use X-rays to view our skeletal structures.

A very small portion of the electromagnetic spectrum makes up the spectrum of light that we can see. Visible light has wavelengths between 3.8×10^{-7} and 7.6×10^{-7} nanometer (nm). The visible spectrum can be broken into colors, which creates the rainbow: red, orange, yellow, green, blue, indigo, and violet. Red light has the shortest wavelength of all visible light and violet light has the longest. Although visible light allows us to see colors, wavelengths within this range do not generally produce heat, and they are not capable of penetrating through most solids.

The wavelength of infrared radiation falls between 7.6×10^{-7} and 0.001 nm. Infrared light falls just beyond red light in the visible spectrum. Infrared radiation carries a great deal of heat energy. While infrared light cannot be seen with the naked eye, it is often used to view people and other living organisms at night using special binoculars or goggles that detect heat, or infrared radiation. Figure 2 shows what someone looks like through heat-detecting goggles.

Figure 2

Infrared goggles allow people to see in the dark.

Connections

When you look up into the sky on a clear night, you can see thousands of stars. However, our universe contains billions of objects that we cannot see with our eyes alone. Many objects in space give off electromagnetic radiation that is not within the visible spectrum. Astronomers use many of the different wavelengths within the electromagnetic spectrum to study space; one of the most commonly used wavelengths is infrared.

Using devices that detect infrared wavelengths, astronomers have learned a tremendous amount about the universe. Infrared radiation is released by stars, planets, and other objects in space that are not hot or powerful enough to emit visible light, or that may be overpowered by nearby bright stars. Additionally, infrared radiation along with many other wavelengths of electromagnetic radiation can be used to track the movement of stars and galaxies. Objects that are moving closer to the Earth emit frequencies that have shorter wavelengths and are said to be undergoing a "blueshift," whereas those that are moving away from the Earth produce longer wavelengths and are undergoing a "redshift."

Want to Know More?
See appendix for Our Findings.

Further Reading

Cool Cosmos. "Herschel Discovers Infrared Light," NASA, March 15, 2009. Available online. URL: http://coolcosmos.ipac.caltech.edu/cosmic_classroom/classroom_activities/herschel_bio.html. Accessed April 7, 2009. This Web site discusses the experiment in which German-born British musician and astronomer Sir Frederick William Herschel (1738–1822) demonstrated the existence of infrared energy.

Imagine the Universe. "Electromagnetic Spectrum," NASA, January 12, 2009. Available online. URL: http://imagine.gsfc.nasa.gov/docs/science/know_l1/emspectrum.html. Accessed March 15, 2009. This Web site describes the types of energy found in the electromagnetic spectrum.

Rader's Physics4Kids! "Light and Optics," 2009. Available online. URL: http://www.physics4kids.com/files/light_visible.html. Accessed March 15, 2009. This Web site explains the basics of visible light and has links to other types of electromagnetic radiation.

2. Coronal Ejections

Topic

The size and speed of coronal mass ejections can be determined from photographs.

Introduction

The Sun, a huge ball of superheated gases that produces light and energy through chemical reactions, is a vital source of energy that sustains life on Earth. At the Sun's core, hydrogen atoms are constantly being fused to form atoms of helium. This reaction releases large amounts of radiation as gamma rays and highly energized subatomic particles. The chemical reactions occurring within the core of the Sun create different layers of gas, each with different temperatures and unique chemical properties.

The *corona*, one of the hottest layers of the Sun, exists in its outer atmosphere (see Figure 1). Temperatures in the corona can reach several million Kelvin (K), a drastic increase from the temperatures on the Sun's surface. This atmospheric layer is composed of *plasma*, ionized gases

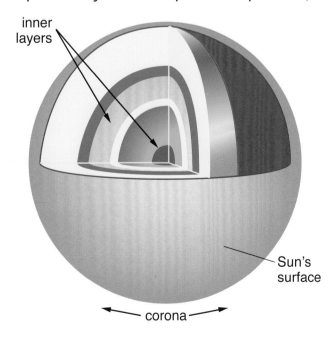

Figure 1

in which some electrons have been stripped from the atoms. The high-energy gases that make up the corona contribute to its uneven and often unpredictable nature. *Solar flares*, *solar loops*, and *coronal mass ejections* of plasma and magnetic energy are fairly common in the corona. These emissions cause a chain reaction that transmits heat and magnetic energy through the Sun. Energy released by the Sun can affect the entire solar system.

The Sun's corona can be best viewed during solar eclipses, when the center of the Sun is blocked (Figure 2). During these times, scientists study coronal emissions to determine their speed and effects on the Earth. In this experiment, you will observe several pictures of solar mass ejections and determine their speed.

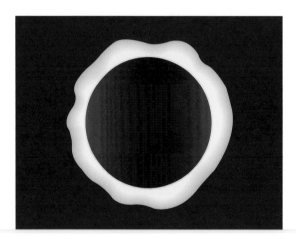

Figure 2

The Sun's corona during a solar eclipse.

Time Required

45 minutes

Materials

- metric ruler
- calculator

❖ access to the Internet

❖ science notebook

| Safety Note | Please review and follow the safety guidelines at the beginning of this volume. |

Procedure

1. Use the Internet to find time-lapse images of four to six successive photographs of a coronal mass ejection. The images you select should include a time-stamp indicating when the picture was taken. One good place to locate such images is on the following SOHO (Solar and Heliospheric Observatory) Web page: images.http://sohowww. nascom.nasa.gov/classroom/lessons/rdat_cme_imgs.html.

2. Choose a feature that you can see in all pictures (such as the outer loop of the solar emission).

3. Measure the diameter of the Sun in each picture. Record your measurements to the nearest millimeter (mm) on the data table.

4. Measure the distance between the edge of the Sun and the feature that you are observing. Record your measurements to the nearest millimeter on the data table. Repeat this measurement for the remaining pictures and record them on the data table.

5. Determine the actual distance between the measured point of the solar mass emission and the surface of the Sun for each picture using the following equation:

$$\frac{\text{diameter}_{measured}}{\text{diameter}_{actual}} = \frac{\text{distance}_{measured}}{\text{distance}_{actual}}$$

- The actual diameter of the Sun is 1.4×10^6 kilometers (km) (865,000 miles [mi]).
- Convert all millimeter measurements to kilometers (1 km = 1 million mm)

Record your calculations on the data table.

6. Calculate the velocity of the coronal mass emission between image 1 and image 2 by dividing the distance traveled by the difference in time between the two photographs, as follows:

$$\text{velocity} = \frac{\text{distance}_{\text{image 2}} - \text{distance}_{\text{image 1}}}{\text{time}_{\text{image 2}} - \text{time}_{\text{image 1}}}$$

Repeat for the intervals between the remaining images. Show all calculations in your science notebook. Record the velocities on the data table.

7. Calculate the acceleration (change in velocity over time) for the mass ejection at each interval using the following equation:

$$\text{acceleration} = \frac{\text{velocity}_2 - \text{velocity}_1}{\text{time}_2 - \text{time}_1}$$

Repeat for all time intervals. Record your findings on the data table.

Analysis

1. Calculate an average velocity for the coronal mass ejection by adding all of the velocities on the data table and dividing by the total number of velocities.

2. The Earth is approximately 150 million km (90 million mi) from the Sun. Assuming that the mass emission maintains a constant velocity, how long would it take for it to reach Earth?

3. Calculate the average acceleration of the mass ejection by adding all of the acceleration figures together and dividing by the total number of figures (5).

4. Is the mass ejection speeding up (acceleration > 0), slowing down (acceleration < 0), or staying the same (acceleration = 0)?

What's Going On?

Coronal mass ejections are very large bubbles of gas that are propelled from the Sun's corona. Although the Sun's corona has been observed for thousands of years during solar eclipses, ejections were not observed until the 1970s because of their random nature. However, using today's technology, the brightest light of the Sun can be blocked by special discs

Data Table						
	Image 1	Image 2	Image 3	Image 4	Image 5	Image 6
Diameter of Sun on picture (mm)						
Actual diameter (km)	1.4×10^6	1.4×10^6	1.4×10^6	1.4×10^6	1.4×10^6	1.4×10^6
Distance from edge of Sun to feature (mm)						
Actual distance (km)						
Velocity	NA					
Acceleration	NA					

in solar photographing devices called *coronagraphs*. Mass ejections from the Sun's corona happen randomly, varying from once within a week to two to three times within a day. Because of the immense amount of material released from the Sun's surface during an event, a coronal mass ejection can generally be tracked for several hours.

Although well studied, coronal mass ejections are not completely understood. Scientists know the causes and mechanisms of these phenomena, but are still unable to predict their occurrence and magnitude. The ejections carry massive bubbles of superheated, charged particles away from the Sun at very rapid speeds, sometimes nearing 1,000 km (km/sec) per second (about 621 mi per second [mi/sec]). An ejection is extremely powerful, having the magnitude of 1 billion hydrogen bombs exploding simultaneously. The electrons within an ejection are aligned so that they propel a very strong magnetic field away from the Sun as they travel. This rapidly moving magnetic flux causes changes in *solar wind* patterns that can affect Earth as well as many other planets within the solar system.

Connections

The Sun's corona is so hot, with temperatures surpassing a million K, that it causes the heated plasma to be propelled rapidly away from the Sun. The plasma moves too fast to be contained within the Sun's gravitational field and is projected from the Sun at speeds as high as 900 km/s (about 560 mi/sec). This hot, rapid movement of particles is known as solar wind. The behavior of solar wind is affected by solar phenomena, including sunspots, solar flares, and coronal mass ejections. The solar wind travels throughout the solar system, creating a bubble of particle movement known as the *heliosphere*, which influences other aspects of the solar system. The solar wind causes magnetic fluctuations within the Earth's atmosphere, creating the *northern lights* and potentially knocking out entire power grids on Earth's surface.

 Want to Know More?

See appendix for Our Findings.

Further Reading

McKenzie, David. "Coronal Mass Ejection Prediction Page," MSU Solar Physics Group, April 12, 1999. Available online. URL: http://solar.physics. montana.edu/press/ssu_index.html#what_are. Accessed March 15, 2009. Dr. McKenzie provides information and photographs about the size and scope of coronal mass ejections on this Web page.

NASA. "Coronal Mass Ejections." Available online. URL: http:// solarscience.msfc.nasa.gov/CMEs.shtml. Accessed March 15, 2009. An animation showing coronal mass ejections on this Web site helps visualize their shape and scope.

Windows to the Universe. "Coronal Mass Ejections," University of Michigan, May 16, 2001. Available online. URL: http://www.windows.ucar. edu/tour/link=/sun/cmes.html. Accessed March 15, 2009. This Web site contains photographs, a movie, and definitions of coronal mass ejections that help explain the concept.

3. Speed of Electromagnetic Energy

Topic

The time required for electromagnetic energy to travel from Earth to other planets can be calculated.

Introduction

The full spectrum of radiation that carries energy through the solar system is known as *electromagnetic radiation*. The characteristics of each type of wave of electromagnetic radiation depend on its wavelength and frequency. Electromagnetic radiation waves include (from longest to shortest wavelength) radio waves, microwaves, infrared light, visible light, ultraviolet light, X-rays, and gamma rays (Figure 1). Shortwave electromagnetic radiation contains more energy than radiation with longer wavelengths and can often have damaging effects. Despite these differences, all electromagnetic radiation waves travel at the same speed, the speed of light: 186,292 miles per second (mi/sec) (ca. 300,000 kilometers per second [m/sec]). In this experiment, you will determine how long it takes for electromagnetic radiation released from Earth to reach different planets within the solar system.

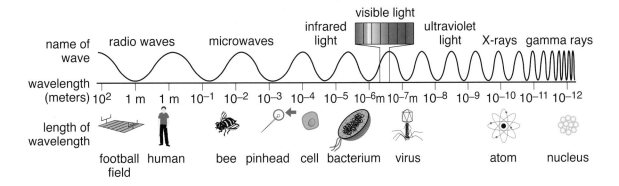

Figure 1

Time Required

45 minutes for Part A
45 minutes for Part B

Materials

- 5 small dried peas
- 2 dried butterbeans
- 1 ball (8-inches [in.] in diameter)
- scale drawing of the solar system
- metric ruler
- calculator
- science notebook

Safety Note   Take care when working outdoors. Please review and
follow the safety guidelines at the beginning of this volume.

Procedure, Part A

1. Follow your teacher to a large outdoor location. You and your classmates will work together to demonstrate the relative positions of the planets and Sun. In this demonstration, one half of a pea will represent each of the inner planets: Mercury, Venus, Earth, and Mars. You will use a butterbean to represent the large outer planets: Jupiter and Saturn. A whole pea will represent Uranus and a half pea the dwarf planet Pluto.

2. Place the 8-in. ball on the ground to represent the Sun. Take 10 paces from the ball. Have a student stand at the 10-pace point and hold one half of a pea to represent Mercury.

3. Take 9 paces from Mercury and have a student hold another half pea (Venus).

4. Take 7 paces from Venus and have a student hold another half pea (Earth).

5. Take 14 paces from Earth and have a student hold another half pea (Mars).

6. Take 81 paces from Mars and have a student hold a butter bean (Jupiter).

7. Take 112 paces from Jupiter and have a student hold a butter bean (Saturn).

8. Take 249 paces from Saturn and have a student hold a pea (Uranus).

9. Take 281 paces from Uranus and have a student hold a pea (Neptune).

10. Take 242 paces from Neptune and have a student hold a half pea (Pluto).

11. Answer Analysis questions 1 and 2.

Procedure, Part B

1. Answer Analysis questions 3 and 4.

2. Using the scale drawing of the solar system, measure the distance from the Earth to the Sun and from Earth to each of the eight other planets. Record these measurements to the nearest centimeter (cm) on the data table.

3. Using the scale on your drawing, convert all measurements to actual distances in kilometers (km).

4. Knowing that the speed of light is 299,792.458 m/sec, determine how long it will take for electromagnetic radiation from Earth to reach the Sun and each of the planets, in seconds.

5. Convert all of the times from your data table (in seconds) to minutes by dividing each time by 60. Record these figures on your data table.

6. Answer Analysis questions 5 through 8.

Analysis

1. How far is it (in paces) from the Sun to Pluto?

2. Do the intervals between planets get larger or smaller as you move from Mercury toward Pluto?

3. What is the halfway point between the Sun and Pluto?

4. Look at Figure 2, which shows the solar system. If it takes approximately 8.3 min. for light to travel from the Sun to the Earth, how long do you think it will take for light waves to travel from the Earth to Pluto?

Data Table

Object	Distance from Earth on drawing (cm)	Actual distance from Earth (km)	Time for waves to travel (sec)	Time for waves to travel (min)
Sun				
Mercury				
Venus				
Mars				
Jupiter				
Saturn				
Uranus				
Neptune				
Pluto (dwarf planet)				

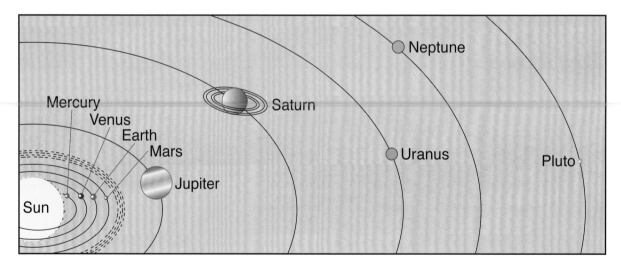

Figure 2

5. Do you think the distance measured from the Earth to the other planets is always the same? Why or why not?

6. Using the measurements from your data table, how long would it take light energy from the Sun to reach the dwarf planet Pluto?

7. Would distance measurement from the Sun to each of the planets be more accurate than your calculations from Earth to the other planets? Why or why not?

8. Why do you think it is possible for waves with different wavelengths and different energies to travel at the same speed?

What's Going On?

Our Sun is a star that is orbited by eight planets and several smaller objects, comets, moons, and dwarf planets including Pluto. Many models of the solar system depict the planets orbiting in a circular path around the Sun. However, some planets circle the Sun in a circular motion, while others move in *elliptical paths*. In addition, planets orbit at varying speeds and in trajectories on different planes (Figure 3). Planets tend to speed up when they are closest to the Sun, and their orbits slow when they are farther away.

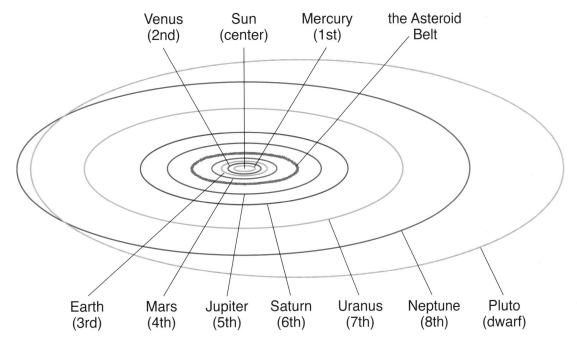

Figure 3

Orbital paths of the planets

Because planets are in constant motion within their orbital paths, it is difficult to predict accurately the amount of time it will take for electromagnetic energy to be transmitted to them from the Sun. For example, at some times electromagnetic radiation waves traveling from Earth reach Pluto in a little over 3 hours, while at other times they take more than 6 hours.

Connections

In the 15th century, Johannes Kepler (1572–1630) studied the orbital paths of planets that rotate around the Sun. Kepler was a mathematician, astronomer, and astrologer who studied the movements of objects within our solar system and distant galaxies. His studies led him to devise three laws regarding planetary motion. Although the foundational thinking behind Kepler's three laws is no longer accepted, his laws and calculations are still accurate with regard to planetary motion within our solar system.

Kepler's first law of planetary motion states that planetary motion is elliptical, with the Sun being a fixed point at the center of the elliptical motion. This accurately describes the motion of all planets within the solar system. Within an ellipse, the sum of the distance from each point within the curve to two different points is always constant. Therefore, the shapes of elliptical orbits vary, as they do within the solar system, but the planets all move in a fixed pattern. Kepler's second law, known as the law of equal areas, describes the speed of planets in relation to their distance from the Sun. Planets move faster when they are close to the Sun and their movements slow when they are farther away. Kepler's third law describes the relationship between the orbits of all planets, stating that their movements are proportional to each other.

Want to Know More?

See appendix for Our Findings.

Further Reading

"The Electromagnetic Spectrum." Hyperphysics. Available online. URL: http://hyperphysics.phy-astr.gsu.edu/hbase/ems1.html. Accessed August 23, 2009. This Web site explains how wavelength and frequency are related.

Enchanted Learning. "The Planets," 2009. Available online. URL: http://www.enchantedlearning.com/subjects/astronomy/planets/. Accessed March 15, 2009. This Web site provides data on each of the planets and diagrams of the paths of their orbits.

Hamilton, Calvin J. "The Solar System," 2005. Available online. URL: http://www.solarviews.com/eng/solarsys.htm. Accessed March 15, 2009. Hamilton discusses the planets, their orbits, and their distances from Earth and from the Sun.

Henderson, Tom. The Physics Classroom Tutorial, "Lesson 4: Planetary and Satellite Motion," 2007. Available online. URL: http://www.glenbrook. k12.il.us/gbssci/Phys/Class/circles/u6l4a.html. Accessed March 15, 2009. Henderson explains the work of Kepler and Newton as it relates to planetary motion.

4. Saturn's Rings

Topic

A scale model can depict the relationship between Saturn and its rings.

Introduction

Saturn is the second largest planet in our solar system and the sixth planet from the Sun. Although not the only planet in the solar system to be surrounded by rings, Saturn does have the largest and most extensively studied network of rings (Figure 1). Galileo Galilei (1562–1642) first noticed a ring around Saturn in the early 1600s; however, he described the structure as "handles" on either side of the planet. Later in the same century, astronomers determined that these handles actually formed a ring. In 1676, the French astronomer Giovanni Cassini (1625–1712) discovered that Saturn had multiple rings with gaps between them. Since that time, scientists have learned a great deal more about Saturn and its system of rings.

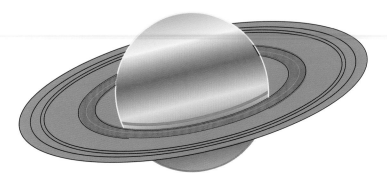

Figure 1

Saturn and its rings

Saturn's brightness and visibility from Earth vary depending on the position of its rings and its location in relation to the Sun. Due to Saturn's rotation, magnetic field, and gaseous composition, the planet's surface appears to be very colorful. In addition to rings, Saturn is orbited by a large number of natural satellites, or moons. In this experiment, you will research Saturn and its rings and then design and build a scale model of this unique planet.

Time Required

90 minutes

Materials

- large Styrofoam™ ball
- cardboard or poster board
- bamboo skewers
- scissors
- tape
- glue
- metric ruler
- drawing compass
- several colors of acrylic paint
- paintbrushes
- calculator
- access to the Internet or books about Saturn
- science notebook

Safety Note   Please review and follow the safety guidelines at the beginning of this volume.

Procedure

1. Access the Internet or use books provided by your teacher to research Saturn and its rings. Determine the diameter of Saturn as well as the width and diameter of each of its seven rings (A–G). Record this information on the data table.

2. Use your research to answer the Analysis questions.

3. Measure the radius (one-half of the diameter) of your Styrofoam™ ball. Record the ball's radius on the data table.

4. Calculate the relative size of each ring in the model by setting up a ratio as follows:

$$\frac{\text{radius of model planet}}{\text{actual planet radius}} = \frac{\text{radius of model ring}}{\text{actual ring radius}}$$

Solve for the "radius of model ring." This calculation must be done twice for each ring for the inside and outside edge. Record the data for each ring on the data table.

5. Knowing the diameter of each ring's inside and outside edges, use a pencil and a compass to draw each of the rings on a piece of cardboard or poster board.

6. Cut out each of the model rings.

7. Insert bamboo skewers into the Styrofoam™ ball to act as supports for the rings.

8. Place the rings onto the bamboo skewers. Secure with tape or glue.

9. Paint your model. You may wish to use a photograph of Saturn as a reference.

Analysis

1. Saturn is known as one of the gaseous planets. Which elements make up Saturn's composition?

2. List Saturn's rings and gaps (divisions) in order.

3. What material makes up Saturn's rings?

4. What forces keep Saturn's rings in place?

5. Is Saturn completely spherical? Explain why or why not.

6. How long is a day on Saturn?

7. How many known moons does Saturn have?

Data Table		
	Actual radius	**Model radius**
Planet		
Ring A (inside)		
Ring A (outside)		
Ring B (inside)		
Ring B (outside)		
Ring C (inside)		
Ring C (outside)		
Ring D (inside)		
Ring D (outside)		
Ring E (inside)		
Ring E (outside)		
Ring F (inside)		
Ring F (outside)		
Ring G (inside)		
Ring G (outside)		

What's Going On?

Saturn's rings were named alphabetically in the order of their discovery. The first rings to be discovered by Cassini were named A, B, and C.

However, modern scientists have discovered 7 rings surrounding Saturn with several gaps between them. With the addition of the new names, the rings no longer correspond to alphabetical order. From the most internal to most external, the rings, gaps, and divisions of Saturn are the D Ring, C Ring, Columbo Gap, Maxwell Gap, B Ring, Cassini Division, Huygens Gap, A Ring, Encke Division, Keeler Gap, Roche Division, F Ring, G Ring, and the E Ring. Figure 2 shows some of the rings and divisions.

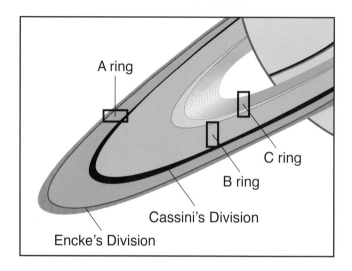

Figure 2

The rings of Saturn are not solid: They are composed of a collection of ice particles, dust, and debris ranging in size from that of a tiny pea to that of a house. All of Saturn's rings are held in place by the planet's very strong gravitational field as well as spokelike structures that have been discovered in recent years. The spokes are thought to be the result of electromagnetic radiation coming from Saturn. In addition to rings, multiple moons orbit Saturn. Sixty of Saturn's moons have been discovered and named to date, some of which can be found in the divisions and gaps between the rings.

The composition of Saturn is primarily hydrogen and helium, along with some other trace gases that circulate around a solid rocky core. Saturn rotates very quickly for such a large planet, completing its rotation in approximately 10.5 hours. Because of its rapid rotation and fluid composition, Saturn is flattened slightly at its north and south poles, creating a bulge at the equator. The atmosphere of this planet is thick with icy clouds that are constantly swirled by strong winds. These fast-moving clouds give Saturn the appearance of having vivid bands.

Connections

In 1997, NASA and the European Space Agency launched the *Cassini-Huygens* robotic space orbiter and probe with the purpose of doing an in-depth study of Saturn and its surroundings. The spacecraft consists of the American-made *Cassini* orbiter containing the European *Huygens* probe (Figure 3). *Cassini-Huygens* flew by Venus and orbited Jupiter before entering Saturn's orbit in 2004. The mission was originally set to orbit Saturn and release the *Huygens* probe for data collection multiple times between 2004 and 2008. However, after four years of gleaning an astounding amount of information and amazing photographs, the mission was extended two more years. The majority of the information that we now know about Saturn is due to the efforts of the *Cassini-Huygens* mission, which is now set to continue through 2010.

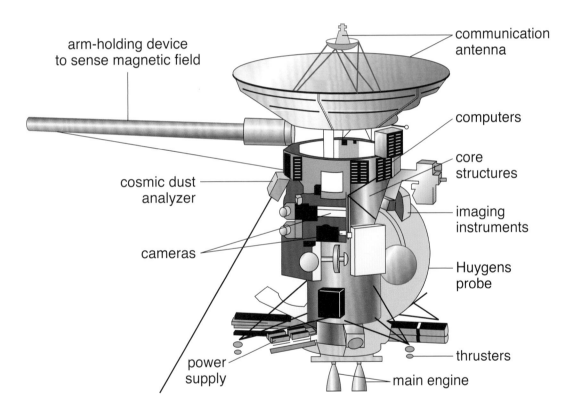

Figure 3

Cassini-Huygens **spacecraft**

Want to Know More?

See appendix for Our Findings.

Further Reading

Hamilton, Calvin J. "Saturn," 2005. Available online. URL: http://www.solarviews.com/eng/saturn.htm. Accessed March 25, 2009. Hamilton discusses several views of Saturn and provides statistics on physical properties, such as mass and density.

Planetary Rings Node. "Cassini's Month-by-Month Gallery of Saturn's Ring System." Available online. URL: http://pds-rings.seti.org/saturn/cassini/. Accessed March 25, 2009. This Web site provides up-to-date pictures of Saturn's rings taken by *Cassini-Huygens*.

NASA. "Saturn," November 29, 2007. Available online. URL: http://www.nasa.gov/worldbook/saturn_worldbook.html. Accessed March 24, 2009. NASA provides information about and pictures of the ringed planet on this Web page.

5. How Efficient Is a Solar Panel?

Topic

Comparison of energy input to the energy output of a photovoltaic cell determines its effectiveness.

Introduction

A *photovoltaic cell*, also known as a *solar panel*, converts solar energy into electrical energy. Solar panels are composed of thin layers containing semiconductors such as silicon. When light strikes these panels, the absorbed energy excites the electrons in the semiconductive material, causing them to move from their original location and generate electricity (Figure 1).

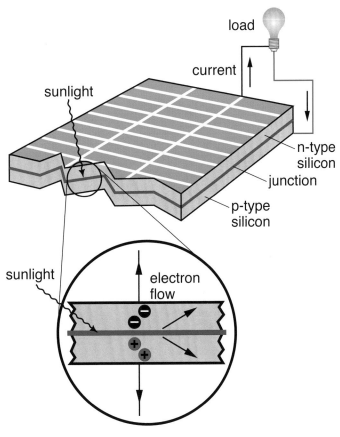

Figure 1

Photovoltaic cell

Solar panels were first invented to harness solar energy in the late 1800s. However, the first photovoltaic cells were only about 1 percent efficient. In the mid-1950s, scientists began using silicon in solar panels, which improved the efficiency to about 6 percent. Today's advanced photovoltaic cells operate with an efficiency of about 20 percent. In this laboratory, you will design an experiment to determine the efficiency of a photovoltaic cell.

Time Required

90 minutes

Materials

- solar lamp
- ring stand
- utility clamp
- photovoltaic cell (solar panel)
- ammeter
- voltmeter
- pyranometer
- insulated wire leads with alligator clamps
- lightbulb with connector wires
- calculator
- ruler
- science notebook

Safety Note   Please review and follow the safety guidelines at the beginning of this volume.

Procedure

1. Your job is to design and perform an experiment to determine the efficiency of a solar panel.

2. You can use any of the supplies provided by your teacher, but you will not need to use all of them.

3. Before you conduct your experiment, decide exactly what you are going to do. Write the steps you plan to take (your experimental procedure) and the materials you plan to use (materials list) on the data table. Show your procedure and materials list to the teacher. If you get teacher approval, proceed with your experiment. If not, modify your work and show it to your teacher again.

4. Once you have teacher approval, assemble the materials you need and begin your procedure.

5. Collect your results on a data table of your own design.

Data Table	
Your experimental procedure	
Your materials list	
Teacher's approval	

Analysis

1. *Pyranometers* measure solar power in watts, while the output of the photovoltaic cell can only be measured in reference to amperage or voltage. So that values can be compared, convert the photovoltaic cell output into watts using the following equation:

   watts = amps × volts

2. What is the difference between voltage, amperage, and power?

3. Determine the solar panel's efficiency, percentage of solar energy that was effectively converted into electrical energy, using the following equation:

$$\text{Efficiency} = \text{solar power} - \frac{\text{electrical power}}{\text{solar power} \times 100 \text{ percent}}$$

4. How efficient was the solar panel you tested?

5. What are the benefits of using solar energy as a power source? What are the disadvantages?

6. How do you think the efficiency of solar panels in converting solar energy to electricity might be improved?

What's Going On?

Photovoltaic cells, or solar panels, are devices that capture energy from the Sun in order to convert it to electrical energy that can be used as a power source. Solar panels contain collections of semiconductive plates that can absorb a certain wavelength of sunlight. As solar energy hits these panels, it excites the electrons in the plates, causing them to move from their original locations. As electrons begin to flow, they are collected and moved out of the solar panel to be utilized as electricity. Solar panels are often used to power calculators and generate electricity within homes. They are also commonly used to power space probes.

Although the efficiency of photovoltaic cells has improved greatly since they were first designed in the 1800s, a great deal of energy is still lost during the conversion from solar energy to electrical energy. Some of the sunlight that hits a solar cell is reflected, returning to the atmosphere instead of being converted into usable energy. Additionally, a portion of the electricity generated from the movement of electrons is lost as heat or is reduced due to resistance or recombination. Although the efficiency of solar panels is generally only around 20 percent, in some cases solar energy can be much more cost-efficient than traditional electrical energy. Depending on the location of the panels, the type of electricity that must be generated, and the amount of sunlight that can be absorbed, the overall benefits of having solar power often outweigh the costs.

Connections

Since 1998, scientists from all over the world have been assembling the *International Space Station*. Even as the assembly continues, scientists on the space station are able to perform experiments and tests for weeks at a time. The electricity required by astronauts and scientists aboard the space station is provided by very large solar panels. (Figure 2). The solar panels on the *International Space Station* are designed so that they will tilt toward the Sun, maximizing their efficiency.

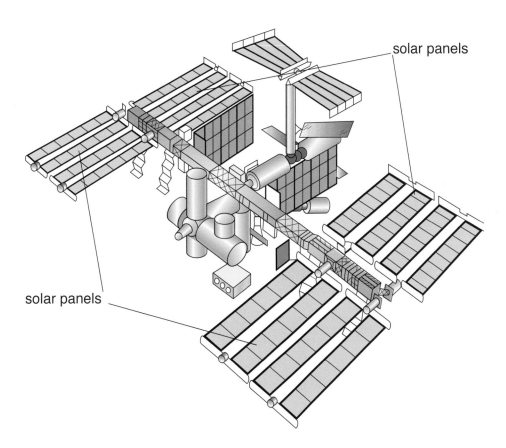

solar panels

solar panels

Figure 2

International Space Station

 **Want to Know More?**

See appendix for Our Findings.

Further Reading

Energy Information Administration. "Energy Kids Page," November 2007. Available online. URL: http://www.eia.doe.gov/kids/energyfacts/sources/renewable/solar.html. Accessed March 25, 2009. Sponsored by the Department of Energy, the Kids Page provides easy-to-understand information and diagrams on solar panels.

Knier, Gail. "How Do Photovoltaics Work?" Science at NASA. Available online. URL: http://science.nasa.gov/headlines/y2002/solarcells.htm. Accessed March 25, 2009. On this Web page, Knier explains how light energy is converted to electricity.

National Renewable Energy Laboratory. "Solar Energy Basics," November 6, 2008. Available online. URL: http://www.nrel.gov/learning/re_solar.html. Accessed March 25, 2009. This Web site describes applications of solar energy.

Tabak, John. *Solar and Geothermal Energy*. New York: Facts On File, 2009. An excellent overview of both solar and geothermal energy and the prcesses by which they can be harnessed.

6. Kinetic Energy of Impact

Topic

The kinetic energy of a meteorite affects the size of the impact crater it creates.

Introduction

Have you ever looked up into the evening sky and seen a *shooting star*? These dramatic nighttime displays are not stars at all but are the result of *meteoroids* entering the Earth's atmosphere. Meteoroids are pieces of metallic rock or debris that range in size from a few inches or centimeters to several yards or meters in diameter. Most meteoroids are broken down by the intense heat that results from high-speed entry into the Earth's atmosphere. However, if part of a meteoroid reaches the Earth's surface, it is known as a *meteorite*.

Meteorites fall to the Earth at such high speeds that they can form *impact craters* when they reach the surface. An impact crater is a large, generally circular, indentation in the Earth's surface. Because of the extreme force of collision, which disturbs the ground around the area of impact, impact craters have a greater diameter than the objects that create them. In this experiment, you will form impact craters using different size balls to represent meteorites and measure the kinetic energy of the balls.

Time Required

60 minutes

Materials

- small plastic swimming pool or similar large plastic container, at least 9 inches (in.) (20 centimeters [cm]) deep
- large bag of sand (enough to fill plastic pool or large plastic container)
- stepladder

- measuring tape
- stopwatch
- 2 metric rulers
- 6 balls of varying size and weight (such as basketballs, bowling balls, and softballs)
- electronic scale or triple-beam balance
- calculator
- access to an outdoor area
- science notebook

> **Safety Note** Use caution when climbing ladders. Please review and follow the safety guidelines at the beginning of this volume.

Procedure

1. Answer Analysis questions 1 and 2.
2. Work with a partner. Place the plastic pool or large container outdoors on a flat, even surface and fill it with sand. Use the edge of a ruler to smooth the sand so that it makes a flat surface. Place the stepladder next to the container of sand.
3. Find the mass of each ball (in grams [g]) and record the masses on the data table.
4. Climb to the top step of the ladder and stretch one arm straight out in front of you. Have your partner measure the distance from the surface of the sand to your hand using the measuring tape. Record this distance in centimeters on the data table.
5. Have your partner place the first ball in your outstretched hand (without moving your hands from their measured distance). Your lab partner should get a stopwatch ready to measure the time (in seconds [sec]) it takes for the ball to reach the ground.
6. Drop the ball into the sand. Your partner should start the stopwatch when you release the ball and stop it when the ball hits the sand. Record the time it takes the ball to strike the sand on the data table.
7. Carefully pick up the ball without shifting the sand underneath it. Measure the depth (in cm) of the impact crater by standing a ruler

in the center of the indentation. Place a second ruler across the top of the crater and note the point at which the two rulers intersect. Record the crater depth on the data table.

8. Use a ruler to measure the diameter of the crater (in cm) and record the measurement on the data table.

9. Move the stepladder so that the next ball will be dropped into a different place on the sand or leave the ladder in place and fill in the crater that you just created and flatten out the sand again.

10. Repeat steps 4 through 9 for each of the remaining balls.

11. Answer Analysis questions 3 through 8.

Data Table					
Ball	Mass (g)	Distance (cm)	Time (sec)	Crater depth (cm)	Crater diameter (cm)

Analysis

1. What factors do you think will affect the size of an impact crater?

2. Which ball do you think will cause the deepest crater when dropped? The widest? Explain your reasoning.

3. Which ball created the deepest crater? Did this ball also create the widest crater? If not, which one did?

4. Calculate the velocity of each ball that was dropped by using the following equation:

$$V = \frac{D}{T}$$

> V= velocity (meters [m]/sec)
>
> D= distance (m)
>
> T= time (s)

5. Use the mass and velocity of each ball to determine its kinetic energy with the following equation:

$$KE = \frac{1}{2}MV^2$$

> KE= kinetic energy (joules [J])
>
> M= mass (kilograms [kg])
>
> V= velocity (m/sec)

6. Create a line graph comparing the kinetic energy (X-axis) of each ball to its crater diameter (Y-axis).

7. What is the relationship between kinetic energy and crater diameter? Explain your answer.

8. How do you think the kinetic energy would be affected if you dropped the balls from your hands without being on a stepladder? From the top of a building?

What's Going On?

All of the solid planets and moons contain multiple impact craters that were formed when meteoroids, asteroids, or comets impacted the surfaces. There are multitudes of impact craters on Earth; however, many of them have either been worn away down by weathering or covered with soil and vegetation. All impact craters tend to have the same basic shape of a central depression surrounded by a rim. In some complex craters, there is also a peak in the center that was caused by the upheaval of soil after collision. Impact craters are also surrounded by *ejecta*, material that was ejected from the crater area. Ejecta can spread out for a great distance beyond the surface of the crater, depending on the energy of impact (Figure 1).

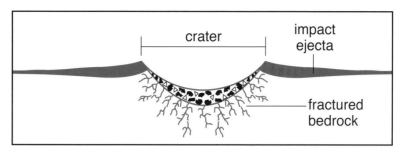

Simple crater

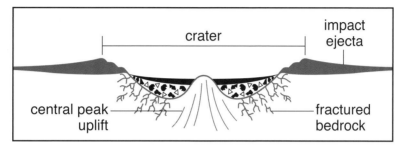

Complex crater

Figure 1

Impact craters vary in size depending on the kinetic energy of the object creating them. Massive meteorites move faster toward the ground and will therefore penetrate deeper into surfaces than small ones. As an object breaks into the surface of a terrestrial planet, the substrate around the area of impact is shifted upward and outward, creating the characteristic indentation, rim, and ejecta. Even though the impact of meteorites can be observed by examining old craters, the actual meteorites are not easily found. Upon impact, the remnants of a meteorite may disintegrate into tiny fragments or be buried far underground.

Connections

Outer space contains much more than just stars, moons, and planets. Many other objects orbit throughout the solar system, including comets, asteroids, and meteoroids. The nucleus of a comet is made up of masses of rock, metal, dust, and ice (Figure 2). The nucleus is enclosed in a cloud called the *coma*. As a comet circles the Sun, it produces a visible tail of dust and gas, which appears as streaks of light across the sky. This "tail" is what distinguishes a comet from an asteroid. Asteroids, also known

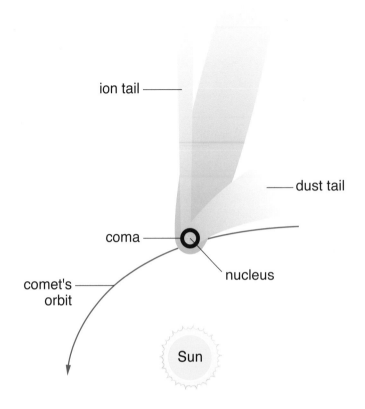

Figure 2

Components of a comet

as dwarf planets, are found throughout the solar system, the greatest concentration of them being in a belt that orbits the Sun in an elliptical motion around the Sun between Mars and Jupiter.

Meteoroids are much smaller, and are often made from debris from comets and asteroids. Meteoroids exist within meteor streams, which are regions containing large numbers of meteoroids that were produced by an impact or movement of some kind. Meteoroids enter the Earth's atmosphere frequently, creating meteor showers. A very small percentage of these meteoroids survive to become meteorites. Although small meteorites impact the Earth frequently, most are not large enough to create a crater and are rarely even noticed. Large meteorites, very rare on Earth, can cause severe damage to the Earth and its inhabitants. Some scientific theories suggest that it was a very large meteorite that caused the dinosaurs to become extinct.

Want to Know More?
See appendix for Our Findings.

Further Reading

Hamilton, Calvin J. "Terrestrial Impact Craters," Views of the Solar System, 2001. Available online. URL: http://www.solarviews.com/eng/tercrate. htm. Accessed April 7, 2009. On this Web page, Hamilton explains how craters are formed and provides photographs of several craters on Earth.

Planetary and Space Science Centre (PASSC). "Earth Impact Database, University of New Brunswick." Available online. URL: http://www.unb.ca/ passc/ImpactDatabase/. Accessed April 7, 2009. This Web site lists all of the impact craters confirmed on Earth, shows the craters on maps, and provides information about each crater.

StarChild. "Comets." Available online. URL: http://starchild.gsfc.nasa. gov/docs/StarChild/solar_system_level2/comets.html. Accessed April 7, 2009. StarChild is a product of the High Energy Astrophysics Science Archive Research Center (HEASARC) at NASA. It provides information for students on a variety of topics in astronomy. This section of the Web site hosts photographs and a video of a comet.

7. A Simple Spectroscope to Identify Gases

Topic

A spectroscope can be used to identify unknown gases.

Introduction

Some of the earliest scientific studies of light were done by English physicist and mathematician Sir Isaac Newton (1643–1747). Newton demonstrated that after light is broken into its *spectrum* by a prism, the colors can be recombined to produce white light once again. Newton was a proponent of the theory that light is made of particles. Other scientists of his time believed that light showed characteristics of waves. It was not until the 19th century that physicists clearly demonstrated the wave properties of light. Shortly afterwards, Noble-prize winning physicist Albert Einstein (1879–1955) showed that light had properties of both waves and particles.

Much of the work of 19th-century scientists who were interested in light was based on studies using *diffraction grating*. This optical device is made up of thousands of tiny slits. When U.S. physicist Henry Augustus Rowland (1848–1901) was doing experiments on the nature of light, he made a diffraction grating by using a fine diamond point to cut about 15,000 slits per inch (in.) (5,905 slits per centimeter [cm]) in a piece of glass. Each aperture in a grating *diffracts* a beam of light into its spectrum of colors. Similar devices are used by scientists today, although the gratings have more than 100,000 slits per in. (39,370 slits per cm).

Visible or white light from the Sun is one of several forms of electromagnetic radiation. Each variety of energy in the electromagnetic spectrum is distinguished by its unique *wavelength*. Long-wave electromagnetic energy includes heat and infrared energy. On the short wavelength end of the spectrum are highly energetic waves, such as X-rays and gamma rays. The waves that contain color, the visible light spectrum, are intermediate on the spectrum (see Figure 1). All electromagnetic waves are measured in *nanometers* (nm), one-millionth of a millimeter (mm). Wavelengths of visible light range from 400 nm (violet) to 700 nm (red) (Figure 1).

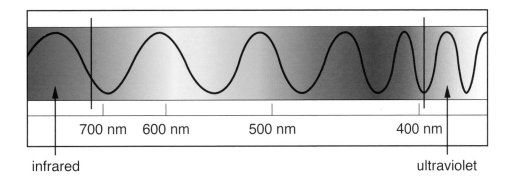

Figure 1

Visible light region of the electromagnetic spectrum

Not all hot, light-producing objects produce the same types of electromagnetic energy. The light from burning objects, such as distant stars, varies depending on the chemical composition of the stars. As elements burn, they produce their own unique signature of energy on the electromagnetic spectrum. *Spectroscopes* are devices that break light from a burning object into its spectrum so that scientists can identify the materials that produced the light. For this reason, a spectroscope can analyze the energy produced by a burning substance and identify the elements in that substance. In this experiment, you will build your own spectroscope and use it to identify the energy produced when different gases are burned.

Time Required

60 minutes

Materials

- spectrum tubes of known gases
- spectrum tubes of unknown gases
- spectrum tube power supply
- old CD (or DVD)
- cardboard box big enough to hold the CD
- 2 single-edged razor blades
- small cardboard tube (from paper towels or toilet paper)

- transparent tape
- aluminum foil
- glue
- pen
- box cutter or sharp knife
- colored pencils
- science notebook

Safety Note Use extreme caution when working with razor blades, box cutters, or sharp knives. Please review and follow the safety guidelines at the beginning of this volume.

Procedure

1. Place the CD on top of the box about 1/2 in. (1.7 cm) from the left edge of the box. Using the pen, trace the inside circle of the CD onto the box.
2. Place the cardboard tube on the box, centering it over the circle that you traced. Trace the outline of the cardboard tube onto the box.
3. Move the cardboard tube over about 1/2 in. (1.7 cm) and trace another circle around the cardboard tube.
4. The overlapping circles that you have traced form an oval. Cut out the oval from the box with the box cutter or knife. This is where the cardboard tube will enter the box.
5. Turn the box one-quarter turn to the right, so that the oval is at a right angle to the table. On the side that is now facing up, trace the inside circle of the CD toward the left edge, as far from the oval cut-out as possible.
6. Cut a small rectangle from the same side of the box as the circle you just traced. The rectangle should be 1/2 in. (1.7 cm) wide and 2 in. (5 cm) high.
7. Carefully unwrap the razor blades and place them over the rectangular hole with their sharp edges almost touching. Carefully tape the razor blades to the box, making sure to leave an evenly spaced, small gap between the two.

8. Turn the box right side up with the top of the box facing the ceiling and the slit formed by the razor blades facing you. Tape the rainbow side (printed side) of the CD to the inside of the box, on the wall opposite the slit. The left edge of the CD and the slit should be the same distance from the left side of the box.

9. Close the top of the box and seal any cracks or holes where light could come in with the aluminum foil and glue.

10. Place the cardboard tube in the oval and wrap aluminum foil around it to keep out light. Adjust the tube by holding the razor blade slit to a light and looking through the cardboard tube. The angle is correct when you can see the full spectrum of colors from red to violet. After you adjust the tube, glue the aluminum foil in place.

11. Your teacher will mount a spectrum tube of a known gas in the spectrum tube power supply. Observe the glowing cylinder of gas through the spectroscope. Write the name of the gas in the left-hand column of the data table. Each of the other columns represents one portion of the spectrum. In the same row that you wrote the gas name, color the columns for the spectrum that you see.

12. View other known gases and record your observations on the data table.

13. View the samples of the unknown gases and identify them based on what you know about the colors of the known gases.

Data Table						
Name of gas	Violet 380–450 nm	Blue 450–495 nm	Green 495–570 nm	Yellow 570–590 nm	Orange 590–620 nm	Red 620–750 nm

Analysis

1. What information can a spectroscope give an astronomer about a star?

2. Describe how you are able to identify the gases that you observed with the spectroscope.

3. When looking at the different light sources through the spectroscope, did the colors fade or blend into each other, or were the colors distinct?

4. Compare and contrast the spectra of the different light sources.

5. How does the light from distant stars and galaxies tell astronomers that the same atoms exist throughout the universe?

What's Going On?

In this experiment, you used a simple spectroscope to analyze the spectra produced by gases. The CD provided the slits required to break light into its individual colors. Although we are most familiar with white light, which includes energy from the entire spectrum, vaporized elements (gases) produced spectra that are unique and can be used for identification purposes.

Chemists use sophisticated *spectrometers* that are much more complex than the one used in this experiment. With a spectrometer, an element is ionized with electricity. As a result, electrons in the element become energized, causing them to move to higher energy levels in their orbits around the nucleus. When the electrons move back down to their original positions, they give off electromagnetic energy. Every element has a unique set of electron energy levels, so the wavelengths produced in its emission spectra are unique. Figure 2 shows the emission spectra of four elements.

Connections

Spectroscopes are used by astronomers to learn about the chemical and physical properties of distant stars. The colors and lines in a star's spectrum are due to the particular elements in that star. Scientists compare the star's spectrum to the spectra of known elements to determine the elements in the star. However, a star's spectrum provides more information than simply composition. It also helps astronomers determine the star's temperature because the color of a star is

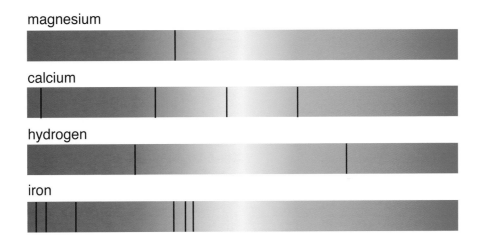

magnesium

calcium

hydrogen

iron

Figure 2

determined by its temperature. The spectroscope can also be used to find out whether the star is moving away from or toward the Earth as well as the speed at which it is moving. The speed can be calculated based on the *Doppler effect*. You have experienced the Doppler effect when you hear the sound waves produced by a moving siren. As the siren moves toward you, sounds waves are compressed and the pitch increases. As it moves away, sound waves are spread out and the pitch decreases. The Doppler effect of light is similar. If a star is moving toward the Earth, the wavelengths of its light are shortened. The reverse is true, so if a star is moving away from the Earth, the wavelengths of its light are lengthened. These changes in wavelength can be detected with a spectroscope.

 Want to Know More?

See appendix for Our Findings.

Further Reading

Dutch, Steven. "Starlight and What It Tells Us," University of Wisconsin at Green Bay, April 1, 1998. Available online. URL: http://www.uwgb. edu/dutchs/CosmosNotes/spectra.htm. Accessed April 11, 2009. In this article, Dutch explains how light from stars can help astronomers understand their characteristics.

"Lab 13: Optical Spectrometer and Diffraction Grating," July 21, 2008. Available online. URL: http://www.unf.edu/coas/chemphys/phys/

physics2/lab/manual/toc.htm. Accessed April 11, 2009. Lab 13 on this Web site is a procedure from the University of North Florida, designed for the advanced student, that explains how to use a spectrometer to identify unknown substances.

Nova Online. "A Self-Guided Tour of the Electromagnetic Spectrum," December 2001. Available online. URL: http://www.pbs.org/wgbh/nova/gamma/spec_flash.html. Accessed April 11, 2009. This interactive Web site explains the different types of energy found in the electromagnetic spectrum.

Walorski, Paul. "How do diffraction gratings tell us information about distant stars and galaxies?" Physlink.com. Available online. URL: http://www.physlink.com/education/AskExperts/ae434.cfm. Accessed August 23, 2009. In this article, Walorski explains how astronomers use diffraction grating.

8. Viewing Jupiter Through a Simple Telescope

Topic

A simple, homemade telescope can be used to observe Jupiter and some of its moons.

Introduction

Jupiter, the largest planet in our solar system, was named by ancient astronomers after the Roman God, Jupiter. While viewing Jupiter through a crude telescope in the early 15th century, Galileo Galilei (1564-1642) viewed four moons surrounding the planet. Since that time, scientists have discovered many more moons, as well as a simple ring system. Jupiter is known as a "gas giant" because it is mostly composed of hydrogen along with some helium and other trace elements. The surface is covered with multiple, complex layers of clouds that rotate in a banded pattern around its surface. One of the best known features of Jupiter is its *red spot,* a huge storm, larger than the size of Earth, that has been going on for at least 200 years.

Since Jupiter is much farther from the Sun than Earth, it takes this massive gas giant a great deal longer to orbit the Sun than it takes Earth. A year on Jupiter is nearly 12 Earth years long. However, Jupiter rotates very rapidly and makes a complete rotation in a little less than 10 hours. Because of this, Jupiter is somewhat flattened at the poles and contains a bulge around the equator. The planet is easily spotted in the night sky since it tends to be the third brightest object after the Moon and Venus. In the Northern Hemisphere, the best time to view Jupiter is early in the evening during the summer (May through September) or in the early morning twilight during the winter. In this experiment, you will create a simple telescope and use it to view Jupiter.

 Time Required

45 minutes for Part A
60 minutes for Part B

Materials

- 2 cardboard tubes that will nest inside each other
- small concave lens
- large convex lens (larger in diameter than the concave lens)
- 2 cardboard or Styrofoam™ squares larger than the tubes' diameters
- hot glue gun
- hot glue sticks
- scissors
- colored pencils or markers
- commercially made telescope
- outdoor location for viewing Jupiter
- science notebook

Safety Note   Use caution when working with a hot glue gun and be careful with breakable glass lenses. Please review and follow the safety guidelines at the beginning of this volume.

Procedure, Part A

1. Use hot glue to attach the small concave lens to the small cardboard tube. If the tube diameter is larger than the lens, use cardboard or Styrofoam™ to make a "gasket" by gluing it to the tube opening than cutting a hole large enough for the lens.

2. Use hot glue to attach the large convex lens to the large cardboard tube. Create a cardboard or Styrofoam™ gasket if necessary.

3. Slide the open end of the smaller tube inside of the open end of the larger one. Make sure that the lenses line up with each other.

4. Hold the end with the small lens up to your eye. Move the lenses closer together or farther apart by adjusting the cardboard tubes until you can focus on an object far away.

Procedure, Part B

1. Use your simple telescope to view the planet Jupiter. Try to find the red spot and look for any moons surrounding it.

2. View Jupiter through a commercial telescope and compare the images to those seen through your telescope.

Analysis

1. Sketch a picture of Jupiter as viewed through your telescope. Color the picture and include any moons that you were able to view.

2. Sketch a picture of Jupiter as viewed through the commercial telescope. Color your picture and include any moons that were able to view.

3. How did the images viewed through the two different telescopes compare?

4. If you wanted to see the side of Jupiter opposite from the one you viewed tonight, how long would you have to wait?

What's Going On?

When Galileo viewed Jupiter, he used a telescope very similar to the one that you created in this laboratory. Galileo was able to view Jupiter's four largest moons: Io, Europa, Ganymede, and Callisto (Figure 1). Each of the moons has unique characteristics:

- Io's surface shows many active volcanoes.

- Europa is covered with a vast sheet of cracked ice.

- Callisto's surface is covered in frozen liquid and solid that has been heavily cratered by meteorites, comets, and asteroids.

- Ganymede, Jupiter's largest Moon, is actually larger than the planet Mercury.

Although the four large moons of Jupiter are the most studied, Jupiter has 24 smaller, named moons.

Jupiter is composed primary of hydrogen around a solid, rocky core (see Figure 2). Jupiter's colorful banded pattern is caused by the rotating layers of clouds in its atmosphere. These clouds consist of many different elements and compounds, including ammonia crystals and ammonium hydrosulfide, which contribute to their vivid colors. Because of Jupiter's rapid rotation, completing one complete turn every 9 hours and 56 minutes, these clouds are constantly in motion. Jupiter's red spot, however, rotates in the opposite direction of the planet. The gigantic atmospheric storm makes a counterclockwise trip around the planet every 6 hours.

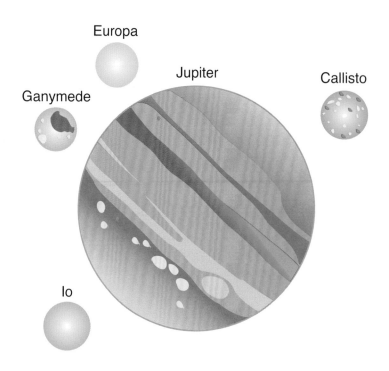

Figure 1

Jupiter and its four moons

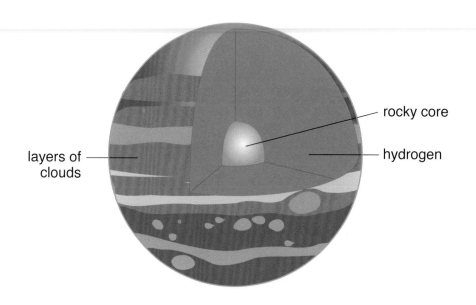

Figure 2

Jupiter

Connections

For centuries, Saturn was thought to be the only planet in our solar system with rings. However, pictures from *Voyager 1* in 1979 revealed that Jupiter has three very thin rings. Years later, satellite photographs showed that Uranus and Neptune also have rings, although Neptune's rings are more arc-shaped and asymmetrical than the ones surrounding the other planets. The four ringed planets within our solar system also happen to be the four that have been deemed "gas giants" because their surface is made mostly of gaseous materials. None of the terrestrial planets are ringed. The reason for the lack of rings on terrestrial planets is unknown and often debated among scientists. Many scientists believe that the magnetic and gravitational energy on terrestrial planets is too unstable to maintain ring structures within their orbit.

Want to Know More?

See appendix for Our Findings.

Further Reading

Baalke, Ron. "The Discovery of the Galilean Satellites," NASA Jet Propulsion Laboratory, April 13, 2003. Available online. URL: http://www2.jpl.nasa.gov/galileo/ganymede/discovery.html. Accessed April 7, 2009. This NASA-sponsored Web site provides information about Jupiter's four largest moons.

Hamilton, Calvin J. "Jupiter," ScienceViews.com, 2002. Available online. URL: http://www.solarviews.com/eng/jupiter.htm. Accessed April 7, 2009. Hamilton provides information and fascinating images of Jupiter and its moons.

Williams, David R. "Jupiter Fact Sheet," NASA Goddard Space Flight Center, November 2, 2007. Available online. URL: http://nssdc.gsfc.nasa.gov/planetary/factsheet/jupiterfact.html. Accessed April 7, 2009. Williams compares characteristics of Earth and Jupiter, including velocity, gravity, acceleration, and density.

9. Sunspot Monitor

Topic

The movement of sunspots can be tracked by daily observations.

Introduction

The first observers of sunspots were probably Chinese astronomers in 28 B.C.E. who viewed them with their naked eyes when the Sun was just rising or setting. When scientists began studying the Sun through telescopes in the 15th century, they confirmed these dark areas, which they described as *blemishes* on its surface. Astronomers later referred to these blemishes as sunspots. Scientists now know that sunspots are regions of the Sun that are dark due to increased levels of magnetic energy. Viewing and studying sunspots helped scientists to realize that the Sun rotates and that it has a variable magnetic field.

The sizes of sunspots vary tremendously. Sunspots are measured in millionths of the Sun's visible area. Small sunspots are only 1 millionth and may be difficult to locate. However, a large sunspot is several hundred millionths. In 2001, an impressive spot measuring 2,400 millionths, fourteen times as large as the Earth, was observed. Although this was the largest sunspot in recent history, it is small compared to the Giant Sunspot of 1947, which measured about 6,100 millionths. Figure 1 shows the sizes of sunspots since 1900.

Monitoring sunspot data throughout history has shown that sunspot frequency varies, but shows peaks of activity approximately every 11 years. These peaks are tied to reversals of the Sun's magnetic field, which take place every 22 years. In this experiment, you will observe sunspots for a period of 1 month.

 Time Required

5 to 10 minutes per day, every other day, for 1 month

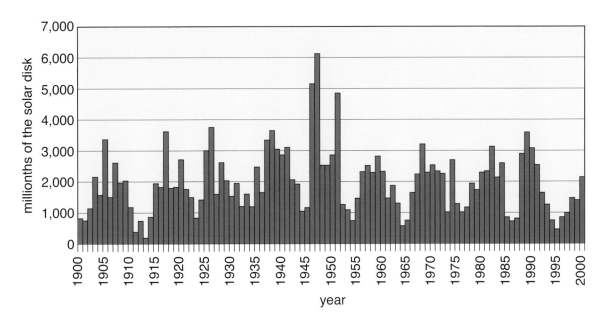

Figure 1

Sizes of sunspots, 1900–2000

 Materials

- telescope or binoculars
- several sheets of white paper
- masking tape
- access to the Internet
- graph paper
- access to an outdoor area
- science notebook

Safety Note   Never look directly at the Sun under any circumstances, especially through binoculars or a telescope, as it can cause blindness. Please review and follow the safety guidelines at the beginning of this volume.

Procedure

1. Tape a sheet of white paper on a flat space in the sunlight, such as the outside wall of a building or a sidewalk.

2. Hold the telescope (or binoculars with one lens covered) so that the wide lens is facing the Sun, and focus it so that the image of the Sun is reflected onto the white paper (see Figure 2). Do not look through the lens to focus it, as it will cause serious damage to your eyes and can result in blindness.

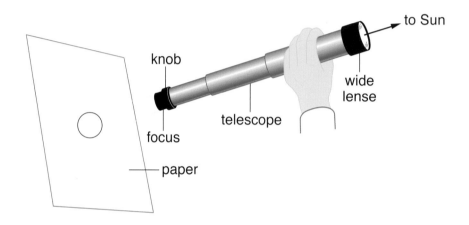

Figure 2

3. Adjust the focus knob of the telescope or binocular until the image of the Sun is very sharp.

4. Hold the telescope or binocular in place and have your lab partner trace the Sun and any sunspots that appear (these will be seen as dark specks within the circle).

5. Remove the paper from the surface and count the sunspots that appeared. Record the number of sunspots on the data table.

6. Repeat steps 1 through 5 at approximately the same time every other day for one month, or until you have 15 readings. If it is cloudy, you may skip a day and then take readings on the two consecutive days that follow.

Data Table	
Time and date	**Number of sunspots**

Analysis

1. What causes sunspots?

2. Create a line graph by plotting the number of sunspots observed each day for the entire month. Be sure to label all parts of the graph.

3. What was the maximum number of sunspots that were observed in a single day? The minimum?

4. Find the average number of sunspots per day by dividing the sum of the sunspots recorded in your data table and by the total number of recordings.

5. Where were most of the sunspots you observed located on the Sun (center, top half, bottom half)?

What's Going On?

Areas of the Sun's surface that are experiencing high levels of magnetic energy appear as dark spots. Magnetic energy prevents normal convection on the Sun's surface, causing the affected regions to be cooler and darker than the surrounding areas. The dark region inside a sunspot is known as an *umbra* and the lighter area surrounding it is called a *penumbra* (see Figure 3). Sunspots can vary in size and shape, but their location on the Sun generally follows a regular pattern that is related to the cycle of dipole reversal within the Sun's magnetic field. The Sun follows a magnetic cycle lasting around 22 years, during which time there are two magnetic field reversals that result in sunspot frequency peaks every 11 years or so. During the first few years of a sunspot cycle, most sunspots appear closer to the poles of the Sun. As sunspots increase in frequency, they are generally larger and can be found closer to the Sun's equator.

When sunspot frequency increases, so does solar activity. *Solar flares* and *solar mass emissions* are much more common in the peak years of the sunspot cycle. Solar flares and emissions can cause electromagnetic disturbances throughout the solar system. Additionally, sunspot frequency can be linked to climate changes on Earth. During the period from 1645 to 1715, there were very few sunspots recorded, and during this time the climate was much cooler on Earth than is typical. This period is sometimes referred to as "the little ice age."

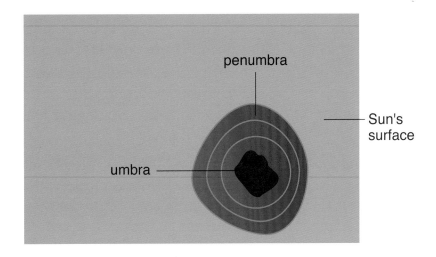

Figure 3

Sunspot

Connections

The outer atmosphere of the Sun, the *corona,* contains superheated plasma that can extend for more than a million miles beyond the surface. The corona can best be viewed and studied during a solar eclipse, when the brightest part of the Sun is covered. The corona is cooler than the core of the Sun, but is much hotter than the Sun's surface. Solar flares and mass emissions occur within the corona. These projections of very hot plasma and electromagnetic energy can impact the entire solar system with magnetic energy. In their studies of coronal activity, scientists have discovered that coronal size, brightness, and general activity are related to the sunspot cycle. As the number of sunspots increase, so does the frequency of solar flaring. In fact, when sunspot numbers are at their minimum, the corona is almost invisible during a solar eclipse.

Want to Know More?

See appendix for Our Findings.

Further Reading

Exploratorium. "Sunspots," Museum of Science, Arts, and Human Perception. Available online. URL: http://www.exploratorium.edu/sunspots/. Accessed April 7, 2009. This Web site describes sunspots and provides photographs of the Sun from the Solar and Heliospheric Observatory (SOHO).

NASA, Solar Physics. "The Sunspot Cycle," April 2, 2009. Available online. URL: http://solarscience.msfc.nasa.gov/SunspotCycle.shtml. Accessed April 7, 2009. This Web site explains sunspots and their cycles.

Phillips, Tony. "Safe Sunwatching," spacewatching.com. Available online. URL: http://www.spaceweather.com/sunspots/doityourself.html. Accessed April 7, 2009. Techniques for observing the Sun are explained on this Web site.

10. How Does Light Intensity Vary With Distance?

Topic

A laboratory procedure can show how light intensity varies with distance.

Introduction

In the solar system, the source of light is the Sun. Each planet is a different distance from the Sun so each receives different amounts of light. The brightness, or *luminance*, of sunlight or any type of light decreases as you move farther away from a light source. Luminance is measured in units known as *candela*.

To learn how distance affects the brightness of light, you can carry out studies using a lamp and a light meter, a device that measures the *illuminance* of light, the amount of light that is hitting a particular surface. Illuminance is measured in *lux*. In this laboratory, you will measure light intensity and then design an experiment to determine how light intensity varies with distance from the source.

Time Required

60 minutes

Materials

- lamp with 75- to 100-watt bulb
- large cardboard box
- aluminum foil
- digital light meter
- ruler
- graph paper
- science notebook

Safety Note   Please review and follow the safety guidelines at the beginning of this volume.

Procedure

1. Your job is to design and perform an experiment to find out how light intensity varies with distance from the source.

2. You can use any of the supplies provided by your teacher, but you will not need to use all of them.

3. Before you conduct your experiment, decide exactly what you are going to do. Write the steps you plan to take (your experimental procedure) and the materials you plan to use (materials list) on the data table. Remember that you should control for all *variables* except the one you are testing, the effect of distance on light intensity.

4. Show your procedure and materials list to the teacher. If you get teacher approval, proceed with your experiment. If not, modify your work and show it to your teacher again.

5. Once you have teacher approval, assemble the materials you need and begin your procedure.

6. Collect your results on a data table of your own design.

Analysis

1. Describe the variables that you controlled in your experiment.

2. Why is it necessary to control variables in a scientific experiment?

3. Create a graph of your results, showing how light intensity is affected by the distance from the light source.

4. The relationship between distance and amount of light intensity can be stated mathematically with the equation, $1/r^2 = I$, where r is the radius, or distance from the light source and I is the intensity of light. Using the distances from the light source as r, calculate the light intensity for each of your trials.

5. Do the results on your data table agree with your calculated results from Analysis question 4? Why or why not?

6. Light intensity is only one factor that affects planetary temperatures. Suggest some other factors.

Data Table	
Your experimental procedure	
Your materials list	
Teacher's approval	

What's Going On?

When a light shines, it radiates in every direction from its source. Near its source, *photons* of light are concentrated in a small area. However, as light moves farther from the source, it has more area to cover and the light disperses evenly throughout the space it covers. Therefore, as the distance increases, fewer photons of light are detected because they are spread out farther from each other than they originally were when released from their source. This relationship, known as the *inverse square law*, explains how the intensity of light decreases in regular intervals as the distance from the source increases (Figure 1). The intensity of light can be related to the distance from its source by the equation $1/r^2 = I$. As the distance from the light source increases, the light intensity decreases exponentially (Figure 2).

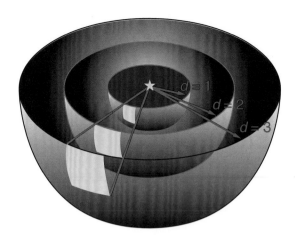

Figure 1

How light intensity varies as distance from the source increases

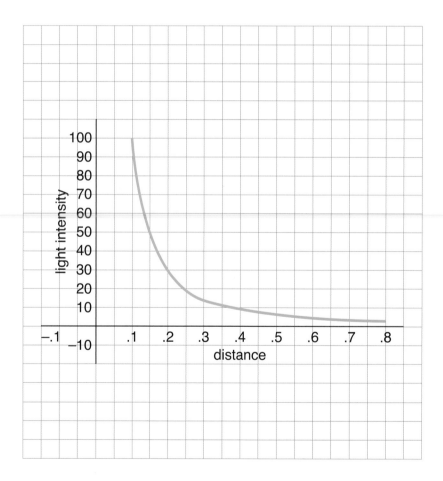

Figure 2

Light intensity decreases exponentially with distance from the light source.

Connections

The Sun provides a source of light and energy for all of the planets in our solar system. The Sun is extremely hot, and the light and heat energy that travels from it influences the temperature of the planets. Because light intensity decreases with increased distance, you might assume that the temperatures of the planets will decrease along with the light intensity. However, this is not the case for all of the planets in our solar system. Mercury is the closest planet to the Sun, but it is not the hottest. The temperatures on Venus, the second planet from the Sun, far exceed those on Mercury (Figure 3).

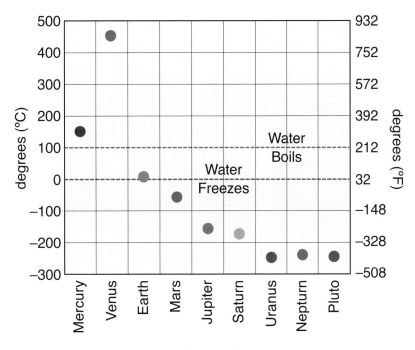

Figure 3

Average temperatures of the planets and dwarf planet Pluto

There are several reasons for this planetary temperature anomaly. First, Mercury rotates so slowly that the side facing away from the Sun is much cooler than the one facing the Sun, which causes the average planetary temperatures to be lower than expected. Second, Venus has a very thick atmosphere with dense clouds that retain heat and cause convection on the planet's surface. This retention of heat dramatically increases the planetary temperature. Aside from Venus, most of the planets' temperatures seem to decrease with their distance from the Sun, but not in the manner that light intensity does. The temperatures on Jupiter and

Saturn are fairly similar even though Saturn is much farther from the Sun than Jupiter. The temperatures on Uranus, Neptune, and the dwarf planet Pluto are also fairly comparable. In the cases of these distant plants, cloudy atmospheres that retain heat and heat-producing cores stabilize the surface temperatures.

Want to Know More?

See appendix for Our Findings.

Further Reading

Fix, John D. "Astronomy Animations," McGraw-Hill, 2004. Available online. URL: http://highered.mcgraw-hill.com/sites/0072482621/student_view0/animations.html#. Accessed April 7, 2009. This Web site provides animations on several topics in astronomy, including the inverse square law.

NASA, Goddard Space Flight Center. "More on Brightness as a Function of Distance," January 30, 2006. Available online. URL: http://imagine.gsfc.nasa.gov/YBA/M31-velocity/1overR2-more.html. Accessed April 7, 2009. The figure in this article clearly shows the relationship between distance and light intensity.

Pogge, Richard. Astronomy 161. "Intensity: The Inverse Square Law." Available online. URL: http://csep10.phys.utk.edu/astr162/lect/light/intensity.html. Accessed April 7, 2009. This Web site, by Professor Pogge of Ohio State University, graphically shows the inverse square law.

11. Flashlight Magnitude

Topic

The apparent magnitude of an object is affected by distance.

Introduction

If you have ever studied the night sky, you know that some stars are brighter than others. The brightness of a star is measured in magnitude. Brightness and magnitude have an inverse relationship, so the brighter a star, the lower its magnitude. With each change of one whole number, magnitude increases by 2.512. Therefore, a star that has a magnitude of 1.0 is about one hundred times brighter than one with a magnitude of 6.0. Star charts and star lists specify the magnitude of each star.

Magnitude can be measured in the following three ways:

1. The *absolute magnitude* refers to an object's true brightness, or how bright that object appears if viewed from a standard distance of 32.6 light years.

2. Since viewing conditions are not always the same, the *limiting magnitude* depends on sky conditions at the time of the observation, taking into account the clarity and darkness of the sky. Limiting magnitude is usually used when describing meteors and deep sky bodies.

3. The brightness of an object from Earth is known as the *apparent magnitude*. Stars that are close to the Earth may appear brighter than stars that are farther away, even if the farthest stars are actually the brightest.

Figure 1 shows a starmap of the Little Dipper constellation with the apparent magnitudes written beside the stars. In this experiment, you will use flashlights to determine how distance affects apparent magnitude.

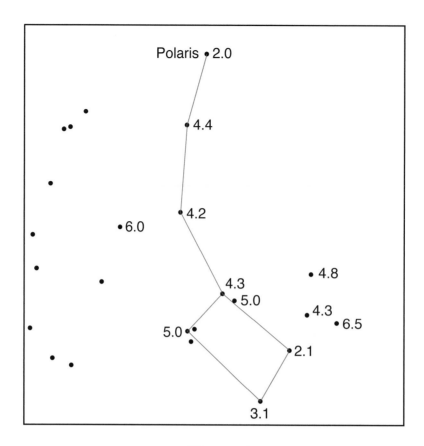

Figure 1

Apparent magnitude of stars in the Little Dipper

Time Required

45 minutes

Materials

- 4 flashlights of various sizes
- meterstick
- access to a darkened room
- labels
- 10 stick-on stars
- science notebook

Procedure

1. Work with a partner. Hold two flashlights and give the other two flashlights to your partner. In a darkened room, you and your partner stand about 6.5 feet (ft) (2 meters [m]) from a blank wall. Turn on all four flashlights and shine them on the wall.

2. Identify the flashlight that shines the brightest and assign it a magnitude of 1. Stick one star on this flashlight.

3. Rate the magnitudes of the other three flashlights by comparing them to the brightest light. Label the flashlights as follows:

   two stars on the flashlight with the second greatest magnitude.

   three stars on the flashlight with the third greatest magnitude.

   four stars on the flashlight with the fourth greatest magnitude.

   (Remember, the dimmest light will be assigned the largest number and will have the most stars.)

4. Turn off the two flashlights that had the least magnitude (the two with the most stars) and set them aside. You and your partner are now holding the one-star flashlight and the two-star flashlight.

5. The person holding the two-star flashlight should continue standing where he or she is with the light shining on the blank wall. The partner with the one-star flashlight should back up until both spots of light on the wall have the same magnitude. Record the distance (in meters) between the two flashlights on the data table.

6. Repeat step 5 using the one-star flashlight and the three-star flashlight.

7. Repeat step 5 using the one-star flashlight and the four-star flashlight.

8. Repeat steps 1 through 3 in a room that has a moderate amount of light (a lamp or some of the lights are on). Record you findings in your science notebook.

Data Table	
Distance between one-star light and two-star light	
Distance between one-star light and three-star light	
Distance between one-star light and four-star light	

Analysis

1. Was the flashlight with the brightest light also the largest flashlight? Why or why not?

2. How does distance from the wall affect the magnitudes of the lights tested?

3. Why do scientists have more than one way to measure magnitude?

4. How would you rate the magnitude of a flashlight that produces a brighter spot of light than the one-star flashlight?

5. *Light pollution* is light produced on Earth that is radiated into space. How do you think light pollution affects the magnitude of stars?

What's Going On?

In this experiment, you measured the absolute magnitude of four different flashlights when you shined them on a blank wall. In this part of the activity, you were able to determine which flashlights produced the most intense light energy. When you held one flashlight at 6.5 ft (2 m) and moved backward with a stronger flashlight, you experimented with apparent magnitudes. You also investigated the limiting magnitude of the flashlights when you turned on the room lights.

For most city dwellers, the magnitude of stars is always limited by light pollution. Light pollution brightens the night sky and makes it difficult for us to see the stars. Currently, 99 percent of Americans live in areas where light pollution is severe, and each year, the problem worsens. In some of the country's greatest observatories such as Mount Wilson in southern California, astronomers are finding it difficult to continue their observations. Only by traveling to the countryside, away from the lights associated with cities and homes, can an Earthbound viewer really see the stars.

Connections

About 150 B.C.E., ancient Greek astronomers developed a system for classifying stars according to their brightness or magnitude. This system included six groups; The brightest stars were given a magnitude of 1 and the dimmest were given a magnitude of 6. For example, Sirius was assigned a magnitude of 1.4. With time, astronomers expanded the scale. Very bright objects, like the Sun and Moon, were assigned negative values because they are brighter than magnitude-1 stars. The Sun's magnitude is an amazing -26.8.

Dim objects that were barely visible were assigned a magnitude of 6. With the invention of the telescope, astronomers were able to see objects that had been too dim to be seen by the naked eye. Therefore, they added some categories to the magnitude scale. Pluto, which has never been seen with the naked eye, has a magnitude of 14. Some of the newest telescopes can see objects with magnitudes as high as 30. Figure 2 shows the apparent magnitudes of several objects in the sky.

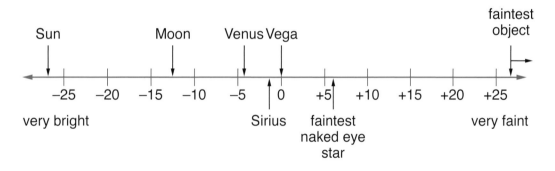

Figure 2

Want to Know More?

See appendix for Our Findings.

Further Reading

Albers, Steve. "Skyglow/Light Pollution." Available online. URL: http://laps.noaa.gov/albers/slides/ast/places.html. Accessed August 23, 2009. The images of the U.S. taken from space on this Web page show areas of light pollution.

Haworth, David. "Star Magnitudes," Observational Astronomy, 1998–2009. Available online. URL: http://www.stargazing.net/David/constel/magnitude.html. Accessed April 28, 2009. Haworth provides amateur astronomers with information on a variety of topics including the magnitude of celestial bodies.

Kaler, James B. "The 151 Brightest Stars," December 22, 2008. Available online. URL: http://www.astro.illinois.edu/~jkaler/. Accessed April 28, 2009. Kaler is a retired astronomy professor who maintains an extensive Web site on all topics related to stars, including magnitude.

12. How Long Is Twilight?

Topic

The length of twilight varies by latitude and time of year.

Introduction

Twilight is commonly referred to as the time between sunset and darkness at night and the time between the first rays of light and sunrise in the morning. Technically, there are three different classifications of twilight: *Civil twilight* is defined as the time between sunrise or sunset when the Sun is 6 degrees below the horizon; *nautical twilight* extends that period until the Sun is 12 degrees below the horizon; and *astronomical twilight* ends when the Sun is 18 degrees below the horizon (see Figure 1). The end of twilight during the evening is known as dusk and the beginning of twilight in the morning is known as dawn.

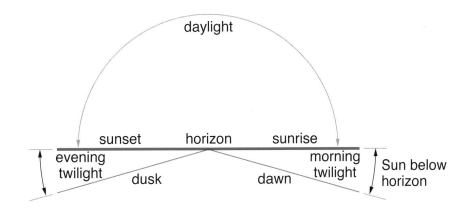

Figure 1

Daylight and twilight

The length of twilight varies enormously depending on the latitude of the observer. Near the north and south poles, where it is dark for most of the winter and light for the majority of the summer, twilight may last for months. At the equator, however, twilight is very brief. In areas between the poles and the equator, the length of twilight varies greatly between seasons. In this experiment, you will measure twilight in the area where you live, then conduct research to compare the length of twilight to other times of year and other locations.

Time Required

10 minutes a day for 2 weeks for part A
45 minutes for part B

Materials

- access to the Internet
- atlas of North America
- graph paper
- colored pencils
- science notebook

Safety Note   Take care when working outside to collect data. Please review and follow the safety guidelines at the beginning of this volume.

Procedure, Part A

1. Working with a partner, set up a schedule for observing the length of evening twilight in your location for a period of 2 weeks. For this experiment, define twilight as the time period between sunset and dark. Since dark is a subjective description, you and your partner must agree on what it means. For example, you could say that it is dark when you are no longer able to read newsprint without artificial light. Or you might say that it is dark if you can no longer distinguish colors. Whatever you and your partner decide will be fine as long as you always use the same standard for dark.

2. Create a data table for recording your observations.

3. Carry out your observations for two weeks.

4. Answer Analysis questions 1 and 2.

Procedure, Part B

1. Use the Internet to visit "The Complete Sun and Moon Data for One Day" maintained by the U.S. Navy at http://aa.usno.navy.mil/data/docs/RS_OneDay.php. This site lets you find out the length of both morning and evening twilight by entering a date and location.

2. Use this site to find out the length of twilight on the dates of your observations. Compare the data to your own findings from Part A.

3. Use this site to find out the length of twilight on January 1, April 1, July 1, and October 1 of last year in your location. Record this information on the data table.

4. Use an atlas of North America to select a city that is several hundred miles north of you. Collect data on length of twilight in this city on the same dates. Record this information on the data table.

5. Use the atlas of North America to select a city that is near the equator. Collect data on length of twilight for this city on the same dates. Record this information on the data table.

Data Table			
Dates	Your location	City to the north	City near equator
January 1			
April 1			
July 1			
October 1			

Analysis

1. Based on your observations, what is the length of twilight in your location?

2. Write a hypothesis that states how latitude affects the length of twilight.

3. Create a bar graph depicting the length of twilight on January 1, April 1, July 1, and October 1 in the three locations you researched. Use a different color for each city. Be sure that all parts of the graph are labeled.

4. Based on your Internet findings, how does time of year affect the length of twilight?

5. Based on your Internet findings, how does latitude affect the length of twilight?

What's Going On?

A day on Earth is 24 hours because that is how long it takes the Earth to make one full rotation. The Earth is tilted on its axis; therefore, either the Northern or Southern Hemisphere receives more intense sunlight. The intensity of the sunlight on either the Northern or Southern Hemisphere causes the four seasons: summer, autumn, winter, and spring. When the Northern Hemisphere is tilted toward the Sun during June, July, and August, it experiences summer (Figure 2). At the same time, the Southern Hemisphere is experiencing winter. As the Earth orbits the Sun, the sunlight intensity changes as the Southern Hemisphere moves closer to the Sun and the Northern Hemisphere moves farther away.

The intensity of light on a hemisphere affects not only seasons and the temperature, but also the length of day and night in that area. During the

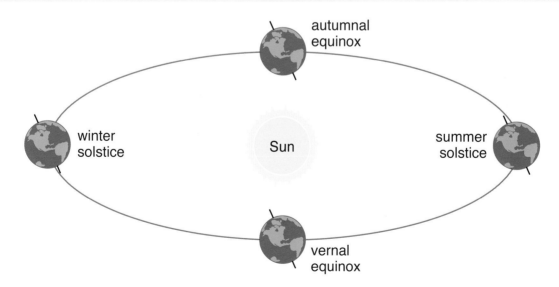

Figure 2

The tilt of Earth on its axis causes seasons

summer months, regions get more hours of sunlight, especially close to the poles. Regions near the north and south poles generally receive 3 months of daylight during the summer and 3 months of darkness during the winter. During the spring and fall, they usually experience about two weeks of twilight. The equator receives a constant amount of sunlight year-round, and since the Sun sets in a perpendicular plane to the area, there is only a brief 20-to-30-minute period of twilight every morning and evening. Areas between the equator and the poles experience different periods of twilight, depending on their latitude. Therefore, twilight length varies by season and by latitude.

Connections

Have you ever noticed that there are more insects and other animals active at twilight than at any other time of the day? Many terrestrial organisms are described as *crepuscular*, meaning that they are most active during twilight hours. Crepuscular organisms avoid being out during the day in order to steer clear of animals that stalk and hunt prey during daylight hours. There are also a great number of skillful nocturnal hunters that only can be found after dark. Therefore, many prey animals, such as deer, rabbits, and insects, enjoy some degree of safety by feeding during twilight hours.

In marine environments, predator-prey relationships are very different than on land. Predatory fish and sharks are generally more prevalent at twilight than at any other time. Large predatory fish have an advantage over their prey during the transition between day and night when underwater visibility is lowered. Therefore, in the ocean and in many freshwater habitats, predators tend to be crepuscular while their prey are either diurnal or nocturnal.

 ## Want to Know More?
See appendix for Our Findings.

Further Reading

Hong Kong Observatory. "Twilight," March 31, 2008. Available online. URL: http://www.hko.gov.hk/gts/astron2011/twilight_e.htm. Accessed May 2, 2009. Civil, nautical, and astronomical twilights are given for Hong Kong over a period of one year on this Web site.

National Oceanic and Atmospheric Administration. "Three Types of Twilight," January 14, 2006. Available online. URL: http://www.crh.noaa. gov/lmk/?n=twilight-types. Accessed May 2, 2009. Clear, scientific definitions of twilight are provided on this NOAA Web page.

U.S. Naval Observatory. "Rise, Set, and Twilight Definitions," September 14, 2007. Available online. URL: http://aa.usno.navy.mil/faq/docs/RST_defs.php. Accessed May 2, 2009. The Astronomical Applications Department of the U.S. Naval Observatory provides information on sunrise, sunset, twilight, and other related topics.

13. Acceleration Due to Gravity

Topic
Acceleration due to gravity can be calculated using two methods.

Introduction
Greek scientist and philosopher Aristotle (384–322 B.C.E.) taught that heavier objects fall faster than lighter objects. His opinion was accepted as truth until the 15th century when Galileo Galilei, an Italian astronomer, physicist, and mathematician (1564–1642), challenged his ideas. Galileo performed experiments in which he dropped masses and measured the distance they traveled and the time it took them to fall. Later, he turned to inclined planes to study the effect of gravity on masses. He concluded that all objects traveling in the same medium will fall at a constant rate, regardless of their mass. Galileo's experiments explained how objects move on Earth and how gravity affects their movements. His work laid the foundation for English physicist and mathematician Sir Isaac Newton (1643–1727), who developed the laws of motion. Galileo is remembered as the father of astronomy because of these ground-breaking ideas and for his improvements to the telescope. In this experiment, you will use both of Galileo's methods to demonstrate acceleration due to gravity.

Time Required
55 minutes for part A
45 minutes for part B

Materials
- large ball of string
- 1 kilogram (kg) mass
- waterproof marker
- bouncy ball (any size or type)
- meterstick

- ❧ access to the top of bleachers (as in stadium)
- ❧ digital stopwatch
- ❧ inclined plane kit (or homemade inclined plane that will support a marble and a baseball)
- ❧ baseball
- ❧ marble
- ❧ science notebook

Safety Note   Take care when working at the top of bleachers. Please review and follow the safety guidelines at the beginning of this volume.

Procedure, Part A

1. You will conduct three trials of a ball drop experiment. Working with a partner, tie the string to the 1-kg mass. Lower the mass by the string over the edge of the top row of the bleachers until the mass touches the ground.

2. When the mass is touching the ground, use the waterproof marker to mark the end of the string that you are holding.

3. Pull up string and mass. Measure the length of the string with the meterstick. Record the distance in the third column of Data Table 1 ("Distance (d)"). The distance will remain the same for all three trials and for the average.

4. Position your partner at the base of the bleachers. From your position on top of the bleachers, drop the bouncy ball (see Figure 1). Start the stopwatch as soon as you release the ball. Have your partner call out when the ball hits the ground. Stop the stopwatch when you hear your partner's call. Record the time of the fall in the row labeled "Trial 1" under "Time (T)"of Data Table 1.

5. Calculate the acceleration of objects due to gravity (g) using the following formula:

$$g = \frac{2d}{t^2}$$

in which *d* represents distance and *t* equals time. Record your calculations for Trial 1 in the last column of Data Table 1.

6. Repeat steps 4 and 5 for two more trials.

7. Find the average for the three trials and record the average on Data Table 1.

Data Table 1			
Trial	**Time (t)**	**Distance (d)**	**Calculation of gravity**
1			
2			
3			
Average			

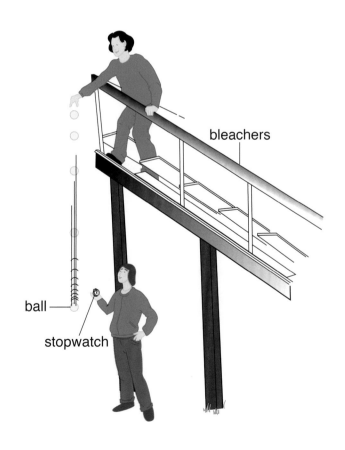

Figure 1

Procedure, Part B

1. You will carry out three experimental trials using a marble and inclined plane. Set up the inclined plane at a 35-degree angle.

2. With your partner holding the stopwatch, place the marble at the top of the inclined plane and release it.

3. Start the stopwatch when the marble is released and stop it as soon as the marble reaches the bottom. Record the time on Data Table 2 in the row labeled "Trial 1."

4. Repeat step 3 for two more trails with the marble.

5. Find the average for the three trials.

6. Calculate acceleration due to gravity using the formula from step 5 of Part A for each trial and the average from Data Table 2.

7. Repeat steps 2 through 6 using the baseball. Record your findings on Data Table 3.

Data Table 2			
Trials (marble)	Time (t)	Distance (d)	Calculation of gravity
1			
2			
3			
Average			

Data Table 3			
Trials (baseball)	Time (t)	Distance (d)	Calculation of gravity
1			
2			
3			
Average			

Analysis

1. Did the marble and the baseball have the same, or nearly the same, acceleration due to gravity? How do you know?

2. The known value of acceleration due to gravity is 9.8 meters per second squared (m/sec^2). Was your average for the acceleration due to gravity closer to the known value when you used the inclined plane or when you dropped the ball from the bleachers?

3. Why is it important to be precise when you measure time in this experiment?

4. Imagine that you have two pieces of notebook paper and you wad one into a ball. You drop both pieces from the same height at the same time. What happens?

5. Why do you think this happens if the acceleration due to gravity is the same for all objects?

What's Going On?

Galileo rolled balls of different masses down an inclined plane and found that the acceleration due to gravity for all of the balls was the same. He may have also dropped balls of equal size, but different masses (an iron ball and a wooden ball) from the top of the Leaning Tower of Pisa to further test his ideas, but no one knows for certain. From his experiments, Galileo developed the concept of acceleration due to gravity, which states that in a vacuum, all objects accelerate toward the Earth at the same rate regardless of size. Of course, we do not live in a vacuum, so air resistance has an effect on how quickly an object falls. However, astronauts on the *Apollo 15* demonstrated Galileo's findings. On the Moon, which has no air, crew members dropped a hammer and a feather. Both struck the surface at the same time.

Connections

Acceleration due to gravity is not the same on all planets. The formula to find a planet's acceleration due to gravity (*g*) is as follows:

$$g = \frac{GM}{r^2}$$

where *G* is the gravitational constant, *M* is the mass of the planet, and *r* is the planet's radius. As you can see in Figure 2, the radii of the planets vary greatly.

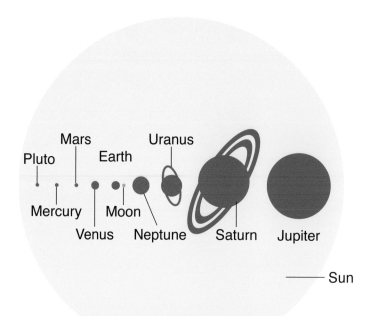

Figure 2

**Relative sizes of the Sun, planets, the dwarf
planet Pluto, and Earth's Moon**

The gravitational constant (*g*) is a known that does not vary from one celestial body to another. The value of *g* is 3.439×10^{-8} cubic feet per slug per second squared (ft³/slug/s²) (6.673×10^{-11} m³/kg/s²). A slug is a unit of mass equal to 14.59 kg. With this information, one can find the acceleration due to gravity on any planet so long as the planet's mass and radius are known. Data Table 4 shows the mass, radius, and acceleration due to gravity (in metric measurements) of the Sun, Moon, and planets. The last column compares the acceleration due to gravity of each body to Earth's. Notice that the Moon's *g* value is about one-sixth of Earth's. On the other hand, the Sun's *g* value is 28 times greater than Earth's.

Want to Know More?

See appendix for Our Findings.

			Data Table 4	
Body	**Mass (kg)**	**Radius (m)**	**Acceleration Due to Gravity, g (m/s²)**	$\dfrac{g}{g - \text{Earth}}$
Sun	1.99×10^{30}	6.96×10^{8}	274.13	27.95
Mercury	3.18×10^{23}	2.43×10^{6}	3.59	0.37
Venus	4.88×10^{24}	6.06×10^{6}	8.87	0.90
Earth	5.98×10^{24}	6.38×10^{6}	9.81	1.00
Moon	7.36×10^{22}	1.74×10^{6}	1.62	0.17
Mars	6.42×10^{23}	3.37×10^{6}	3.77	0.38
Jupiter	1.90×10^{27}	6.99×10^{7}	25.95	2.65
Saturn	5.68×10^{26}	5.85×10^{7}	11.08	1.13
Uranus	8.68×10^{25}	2.33×10^{7}	10.67	1.09
Neptune	1.03×10^{26}	2.21×10^{7}	14.07	1.43
Pluto	1.40×10^{22}	1.50×10^{6}	0.42	0.04

Further Reading

Galileo Project. "On Motion," 1995. Available online. URL: http://galileo. rice.edu/sci/theories/on_motion.html. Accessed May 3, 2009. The Galileo Project provides information on the life and work of Galileo for students of all ages. This page on the project's Web site explains his work on motion.

Kurtus, Ron. "Gravitation and the Force of Gravity," School of Champions, September 2, 2007. Available online. URL: http://www.school-for-champions.com/science/gravity.htm. Accessed May 3, 2009. Kurtus explains the concept of acceleration due to gravity on this Web site.

Physics Classroom. "Free Fall and Acceleration Due to Gravity," 2009. Available online. URL: http://www.physicsclassroom.com/Class/1DKin/ U1L5a.cfm. Accessed May 3, 2009. The Physics Classroom is a tutorial written in easy-to-read language that touches on all topics in physics. This page covers acceleration due to gravity.

14. The Law of Inertia

Topic

The law of inertia helps explain the movement of objects in space and on the Earth's surface.

Introduction

Groundbreaking work by the Italian scientist Galileo Galilei (1564–1642) on the mechanics of motion provided the basis for understanding gravity and the movement of objects on the Earth's surface. One of Galileo's most important ideas was the concept of *inertia*. According to the law of inertia, objects at rest will remain at rest and objects in motion will remain in motion unless an outside force acts on them. In other words, objects resist a change in state of motion or rest.

This concept of motion was not an intuitive one and went against the thinking of the time. Although even a casual observer could see that resting objects remained at rest, it was not so obvious that objects in motion remain in motion indefinitely. Galileo showed how *friction*, an invisible force, explained why objects stop moving. This concept helped Newton develop the first law of motion. In this experiment, you will learn more about the law of inertia.

Time Required

55 minutes

Materials

- 6-foot (1.8-meter [m]) section of 1.5-inch (in.) (about 5-centimeter [cm]) diameter foam pipe
- utility knife
- masking tape
- marble

- cooking spray, WD-40™, or another lubricant
- ruler
- science notebook

Procedure

1. Working with a partner, use the utility knife to cut the foam pipe in half the long way to make two U-shaped sections. Sit on the floor and shape one section of the foam to make the ramp shown in Figure 1. Tape the foam in place, using a desk, table leg, or stack of books to support the foam.

2. Answer Analysis question 1.

3. Hold the marble at the highest point on one side of the ramp while your partner measures the height of the marble (from the floor) and records the measurement in your science notebook.

4. Release the marble and observe it roll down one side and up the far side of the ramp. Have your partner place his or her finger on the highest point to which the ball travels. Measure the distance the marble moved up the ramp. Record your measurement on Data Table 1 under Trial 1.

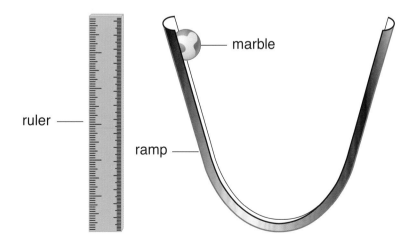

marble

ruler

ramp

Figure 1

Data Table 1		
Height achieved	**Trial 1**	**Trial 2**
First roll		
Second roll		
Third roll		
Average		

5. Repeat step 4 two more times for a total of three times. Record all your results under Trial 1.

6. Average the results of the three rolls and record the average on Data Table 1.

7. Adjust your ramp for Trial 2. Arrange the ramp so that it is more open and the U-shape is wider (see Figure 2).

8. Repeat steps 3 and 4 and record your results on Data Table 1 under Trial 2.

9. Spray cooking spray, WD-40™, or some other lubricant on the ramp. Repeat steps 3 through 8 and record you results on Data Table 2.

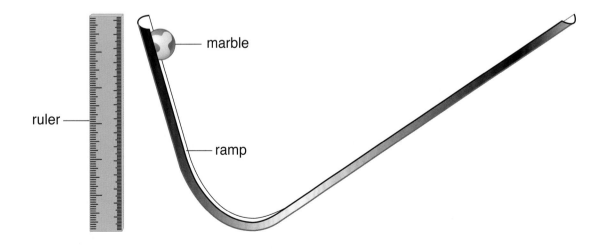

Figure 2

Data Table 2		
Height achieved	**Trial 1**	**Trial 2**
First roll		
Second roll		
Third roll		
Average		

Analysis

1. Write a hypothesis stating what will happen to the marble once you release it from the highest point on the ramp.

2. Based on your experimental results, did your hypothesis prove to be correct? Explain how the experiment supported or refuted your hypothesis.

3. How did changing the shape of the ramp affect the height to which the marble rolled?

4. How did the addition of a lubricant to the ramp affect the height to which the marble rolled?

5. Based on your experiment, what force do you think prevented the marble from reaching the starting height?

What's Going On?

Galileo performed an experiment very much like this one. He saw that a ball released from the top of a U-shaped ramp rolls down one side of the ramp and up the opposite side, just short of the original height. When he reduced the friction on his ramp, the ball rolled up the second ramp to a height that was almost equal to the original. According to Galileo, the difference between the original height of the ball and the height it achieved up the opposite side of the ramp was due to the force of friction. Galileo stated that if friction could be eliminated, the ball would achieve the original height. In another experiment, Galileo wanted to find out how the shape of the ramp affected the ball's ability to reach the original height. He extended one side of the U-shaped ramp at a much lower angle. Even so, the ball reached a height a little short of the original height. Reducing friction enabled the ball to almost gain its original height.

From his experiments, the scientist concluded that if the opposite incline was changed to 0 degrees (see Figure 3), then the ball would roll forever attempting to reach the original height, assuming no friction. In other words, the ball would continue in motion until something stopped it. Galileo's experiment showed that a force was not required to put an object in motion. Instead, a force is needed to stop the motion of a moving object.

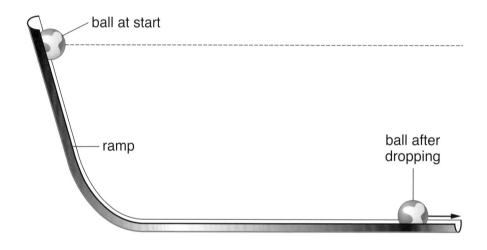

ball at start

ramp

ball after dropping

Figure 3

Connections

Before Galileo, astronomers subscribed to the impetus theory, which said that an object in motion would remain in motion until it ran out of impetus. They saw impetus as a force that moved objects. Galileo's idea was that motion was a natural state for objects, and that an object would continue until something stopped it. We now know that the "something" is friction. On Earth, we never see objects in this state of uninhibited motion. However, Galileo's theory of inertia explains the motion of objects in space.

Want to Know More?

See appendix for Our Findings.

Further Reading

Education in Physics and Mathematics. "Galileo and Inertia," 2006. Available online. URL: http://id.mind.net/~zona/mstm/physics/ mechanics/forces/galileo/galileoInertia.html. Accessed May 7, 2009. Animations on this Web site show how balls behave when moving down one inclined plane and up another.

Physics 30. "Newton's Laws of Motion," Saskatchewan Learning. Available online. URL: http://physics30.edcentre.ca/kindyn/lessoni_6_2.html. Accessed May 7, 2009. Several illustrations and simple explanations give everyday samples of inertia.

University of Virginia. "Phun Physics: Inertia." Available online. URL: http://phun.physics.virginia.edu/topics/inertia.html. Accessed May 7, 2009. This Web site discusses Newton's ideas of inertia and gives good examples.

15. Who Knows Ten Constellations?

Topic

A student-developed survey can assess the student body's knowledge of common constellations.

Introduction

People have always been interested in the patterns created by stars and planets in the night sky. Some of the earliest scientists were astronomers in Mesopotamia, a region between the Tigris and Euphrates rivers in what is now Iraq. Mesopotamian scientists built observatories, routinely watched the sky, and recorded their observations about 6,000 years ago. They marked the arrival of spring by the appearance of a *constellation* named the Bull of Heaven. A constellation is a region of the sky containing a recognizable group of stars. The other seasons were heralded by three different constellations. Eventually the scientists identified eight more constellations for a total of twelve that were collectively known as the *zodiac*.

Today's astronomers recognize 88 constellations in the Northern and Southern Hemispheres. Some constellations resemble animals and have names like Ursa Major, the Big Bear, Cygnus the Swan (Figures 1a and 1b), and Aquila the Eagle. Others represent important people in mythology. Cassiopeia depicts a queen chained to her throne. Gemini represents the twins Castor and Pollux, two Greek heroes. Boötes the Herdsman (Figures 2a and 2b), also known as Boötes the Bear Watcher, received his name because he appears to be watching or chasing the bear Ursa Major across the sky. In this experiment, you will design a survey to find out many students can identify 10 common constellations.

 Time Required

45 minutes on day 1
45 minutes on day 2

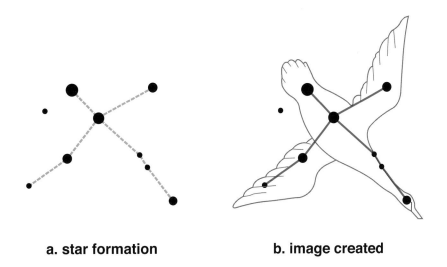

a. star formation   **b. image created**

Figure 1

Cygnus the Swan

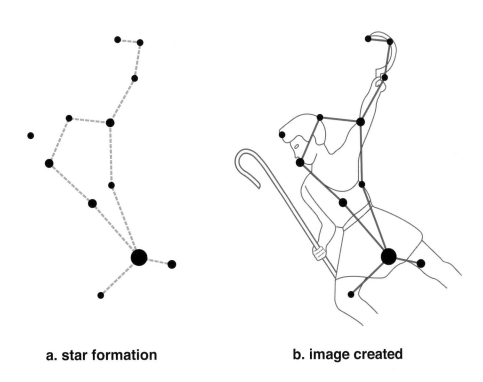

a. star formation   **b. image created**

Figure 2

Boötes the Bear Watcher

Materials

- ⦁◇ access to books of constellations or the Internet
- ⦁◇ drawing paper or a printer
- ⦁◇ science notebook

Procedure Day 1:

1. Your job is to design a survey to find out how many students at your school can identify 10 constellations. As you are designing your survey, keep these points in mind:

    a. You will need drawings or pictures of the constellations you expect students to identify.

    b. You will need a checklist to be completed as students look as pictures of constellations and attempt to identify them.

    c. You should determine how many students you will survey before you begin. The larger your survey group, the more accurate your results.

2. Create a rough draft of a survey plan and questionnaire and show it to your teacher. If you get teacher approval, carry out the survey. If not, rewrite the plan and questionnaire and show it to your teacher again.

Procedure Day 2:

1. Carry out your survey and record your findings.
2. Compile your survey results on the data table.

Data Table	
Name of constellation	**Number of students who could identify this constellation**
1.	
2.	
3.	
4.	
5.	
6.	
7.	
8.	
9.	
10.	

Analysis

1. Why is it important to survey a large group of people?

2. How many students attend your school? What percentage of your total student body did you survey? To find percentage, use the following formula:

$$\text{percentage} = \frac{\text{number of students surveyed}}{\text{total number of students in school X 100}}$$

3. What percentage of the students you surveyed could identify all 10 constellations?

4. Were there any constellations that all students could identify? If so, which ones.

5. Were there any constellations that none of the students could identify? If so, which ones.

What's Going On?

If you observe the night sky, you might have trouble identifying the constellations. Most of them show little resemblance to the figures for which they were named. Ancient astronomers bestowed the names on constellations to honor their favorite people or creatures. Within the 88 identified constellations 19 are named for land animals including a fox, scorpion, bull, peacock, bear, lynx, and wolf; 29 are named for inanimate objects, such as an air pump, altar, compass, and crown, and the rest are named for people, water animals, birds, insects, centaurs, a head of hair, a dragon, a serpent, a flying horse, and a river.

Connections

Although written records from ancient times are scarce, scientists feel fairly confident about the geographic locations of the earliest astronomers. These people identified and wrote about constellations that can be clearly seen from 36 degrees north, the regions of Mesopotamia and Babylonia. The observers did not see any constellations in the Southern Hemisphere, which was apparently below their line of sight. From their origins, information of constellations spread to Greece and Egypt. In 150 c.e., Egyptian scientist Ptolemy (circa 100–170 c.e.) printed a book that included information on 48 constellations. These constellations formed the basis of today's constellation system. Over time, knowledge of astronomy spread to other countries and scientists added their own discoveries. New constellations were discovered by Dutch cartographer Gerardus Mercator (1512–94) in 1551, and Dutch explorer and navigators Pieter Keyser (1540–96) and Frederik de Houtman (1571–1627) in the early 1600s. Other major contributors include the Polish astronomer Johannes Hevelius (1642–45) and French astronomer Nicolas Louis de Lacaille (1713–62).

Want to Know More?

See appendix for Our Findings.

Further Reading

Dibon-Smith, Richard. "The Constellations," February 10, 2009. Available online. URL: http://www.dibonsmith.com/menu.htm. Accessed May 22, 2009. Dibon-Smith provides detailed information on the major constellations, including the names of the stars in each.

Kronberg, C. "Constellations," September 7, 2000. Available online. URL: http://seds.org/Maps/Const/constS.html. Accessed August 13, 2009. This Web site provides two photographs of each constellation, one with an outline and one without.

Legg Middle School Planetarium. "Constellation Mythology." Available online. URL: http://www.coldwater.k12.mi.us/lms/planetarium/myth/index.html. Accessed May 22, 2009. Links to constellations are provided in this Web site. Each link includes drawings and information on the constellation.

16. The Size of the Universe

Topic

Distances in the universe can be visualized on a smaller scale.

Introduction

When you look at the night sky, you can see planets, stars, and even distant galaxies. However, you cannot discern how far away these objects are from Earth. Distances between objects in space are enormous, much too large to be measured directly. Astronomers get their measurements indirectly using the *parallax effect*, the apparent displacement of a stationary object against a background when the object is viewed from two different points. The amount that the object seems to move (or shift) is due to the distance to the object and the distance between the two points of observation. Through the parallax effect and other types of indirect measurements, astronomers have calculated the distances from Earth to the objects listed on the data table.

Notice that the data table shows distances in light years (ly). Light travels at the incredible speed of 186,000 miles/second (mi/sec)(299,792,458 meters/second [m/sec]). In one year, a beam of light can travel 5,865,696,000,000 miles (mi) (9,460,800,000,000 kilometers [km]). This means that if you see an object that is 1 ly away, the light reaching your eyes left that object 1 year ago. In this experiment, you are going to develop a scale using metric measurements that shows the relative distances between Earth and several objects in space.

Time Required

55 minutes

Materials

- meterstick

- 9 index cards, small sheets of paper, or other objects (to represent celestial objects)

- colored pencils

- tape

- paper clips

- science notebook

Safety Note Please review and follow the safety guidelines at the beginning of this volume.

Procedure

1. Examine the data table, which shows the distances from Earth to several celestial objects in the universe, including stars and galaxies. Distances are given in light years. Notice that the Moon, Sun, and planets are not on this data table. They are all less than 1 ly from Earth.

2. Your assignment is to develop a workable distance scale on which you can show the relative distances of far celestial objects from Earth. For example, you might let 1 centimeter (cm) represent 100 ly. If you use this scale, the center of the Milky Way will be 3.8 m from Earth. Or, you could let 1 cm represent 10 ly, in which case the Milky Way would be 38 m from Earth. You are only required to show 8 of the objects listed on the data table.

3. Once you have selected a scale, cut a piece of string that can represent the entire distance scale.

4. Decide which of the celestial objects you are going to show on the distance scale. You may use index cards, drawings, or any other objects to represent the celestial objects along the string.

5. Attach the cards, drawings, or other objects at the appropriate points on the string, which represents the entire scale (see Figure 2).

Data Table

Celestial object	Description of object	Distance from Earth in light years (ly)
Alpha Centauri	Alpha Centauri is the nearest star to Earth.	4.27
Sirius	The brightest star in the sky, Sirius is a member of the constellation Canis Major and is also called the Dog Star (Figure 1).	8.7
Arcturus	Arcturus is a bright star in the constellation Boötes.	36
Pleiades Cluster	This cluster of about 100 stars is also called the Seven Sisters.	400
Betelgeuse	In the constellation Orion, Betelgeuse is the second brightest star.	520
Deneb	Deneb is the brightest star in the constellation Cygnus.	1,600
Crab Nebula	This cloud of cosmic dust and gas is the remnant of a star that exploded in 1054.	4,000
Center of Milky Way	Our solar system is the Milky Way, which contains about a half trillion stars.	38,000
Magellanic Clouds	These are small galaxies relatively close to our Milky Way.	150,000
Andromeda Galaxy	The Andromeda Galaxy is a close neighbor that is structurally similar to the Milky Way.	2,200,000

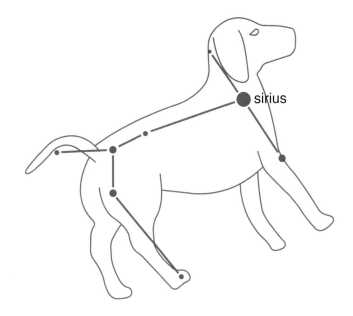

Figure 1

Sirius the Dog Star is in the constellation Canis Major.

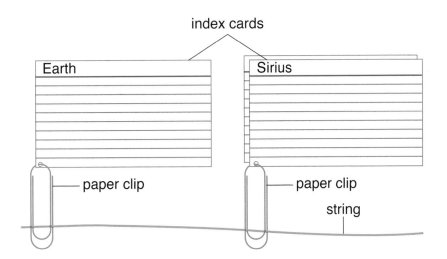

Figure 2

Analysis

1. On your distance scale, what represents 100 ly?

2. The Moon is 240,000 mi (386,242 km) from Earth. Why could the Moon not be included on your distance scale?

3. Explain how viewing a star that is 10 ly away is like looking into the past.

4. Light from the Sun travels 8.4 minutes (min) to reach the Earth. Knowing that light travels at 186,000 mi/sec, calculate the distance of the Sun from the Earth.

5. Is it possible to see galaxies that are so distant from us that their light has not reached Earth? Explain your answer.

What's Going On?

Visualizing astronomical distances is very difficult because we do not experience them here on Earth. Suppose that you are on an imaginary rocket that travels at 60 miles per hour (mph) (about 96 kilometers per hour [kph]), average highway speed. If you left Earth and traveled to the Sun without stopping for any breaks, you would arrive in 180 years! Light makes that trip in only 8 min.

Creating a distance scale of objects in the universe puts some perspective on the tremendous size of space. When you are working with light years, "near" and "far" take on different meanings. You were not able to put the Sun, Moon, and planets on your scale because they are very close to us compared to other objects in space. Traveling at the speed of light, you could reach the Moon in 1.2 sec! Venus, our closest planet, is only 2.5 light minutes away.

On this type of scale, looking at distance is the same as looking at time travel. When we see light from a distant object, we are seeing that object in the past. When we see distant galaxies, we are viewing light that left those galaxies millions of years ago. For us to see those objects as they are now, we would have to travel to them at a speed faster than light. According to Albert Einstein's theory of relativity, nothing can travel faster that light. Some galaxies are so distant that their light has not reached us yet. There could be objects that are so remote that their light will never make it to Earth.

Connections

The universe is about 13.7 billion years old. Consequently, light from the early galaxies has been traveling more than 13 billion years. However, this does not tell us the size of the universe because it is expanding or stretching. The universe began from a small point of matter that underwent a rapid expansion, an event known as the *big bang*. Today's universe is about 1,000 times larger than the original, which means that the universe may have a diameter of 157 billion ly.

Scientists know that the universe is expanding because galaxies are moving away from us. However, the galaxies themselves are not moving like a ball that you have just pitched to a friend; the galaxies are stationary and the space between them is stretching. To visualize this type of expansion, think of two ink dots on a rubber band. When you stretch the rubber band, the dots move farther apart.

Not everything in the universe is expanding. The Earth, Moon, planets, and Sun are not affected by this phenomenon. On the relatively small scale of the solar system, or even our galaxy, the effects of gravity overcome the effects of expansion. Only by looking at the entire universe, which is mostly space, can the expansion of space be understood.

Want to Know More?

See appendix for Our Findings.

Further Reading

Britt, Robert Roy. "Universe Measured: We're 156 Billion Light Years Wide," Space.com, May 24, 2004. Available online. URL: http://www. space.com/scienceastronomy/mystery_monday_040524.html. Accessed May 25, 2009. On this Web site Britt explains how astronomers have calculated the size of the universe.

NASA. "How Fast Is The Universe Expanding?" Our Universe, October 14, 2008. Available online. URL: http://map.gsfc.nasa.gov/universe/ uni_expansion.html. Accessed May 26, 2009. The Web page explains the contributions of Edwin Hubble to understanding the expansion of the universe.

Puchnarewicz, Liz. "The Expanding Universe," Mullard Space Science Laboratory, March 16, 1998. Available online. URL: http://www.mssl. ucl.ac.uk/www_astro/agn/universe.html. Accessed May 26, 2009. This animation shows how galaxies are moving away from each other.

17. Rocket Science

Topic

The weight of a rocket's payload affects the duration of its flight.

Introduction

You know what happens when you inflate a balloon, then release it. The balloon flies around the room for a few seconds before falling to the floor. Flying balloons can give you some insight into rockets and how they work.

Rockets are vehicles that move forward because they eject fast-moving fluid from the exhaust in the rear. The moving fluid gives the rocket *thrust,* a push forward. The faster the fluid moves out of the rocket, the more thrust it gives the rocket. The principle behind rocket propulsion is based on Isaac Newton's third law of motion: for every action there is an equal and opposite reaction (see Figure 1). A rocket's thrust must be strong enough to overcome gravity and get the *payload,* the materials carried on board the rocket, off ground. If there is not enough fluid moving out of the rocket, the rocket will not reach its destination and will crash back to Earth. For this reason, engineers carefully balance the amount of material needed for thrust with the design of the rocket and the weight of its payload. In this experiment, you will find out how the weight of a payload affects the duration of a rocket's flight.

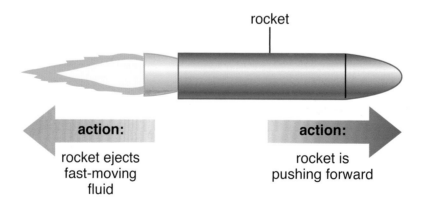

Figure 1

Time Required

55 minutes

Materials

- access to an outdoor area
- airplane glue
- model rocket kit
- launching pad and launcher recovery wadding
- rocket engines
- igniter
- triple-beam balance or electronic scale
- fine-grit sandpaper
- single-edge razor blade
- scissors
- white glue
- black marker
- stopwatch
- small ball of modeling clay (about the size of half a tennis ball)
- science notebook

Safety Note   Only launch rockets outdoors in an open area on a day when there is little or no wind. Do not launch rockets near dead grass or other flammable vegetation. Stand at least 15 feet (ft) (4.6 meters [m]) away from the rocket when launching. Only use the electrical launching devices that come with the rockets; do not use fuses or matches. Make sure that the igniter's safety key is removed when connecting wires and clips. Make sure that the launch pad is stable so that it will not turn over during launch. Adult supervision is required. Please review and follow the safety guidelines at the beginning of this volume.

Procedure

1. Work with a group. Assemble the rocket according to the directions in the kit. Use the sandpaper, airplane glue, white glue, and scissors as needed to help in the assembly.

2. Using the marker, write a number or letter on your rocket to identify it and distinguish it from your classmates' rockets.

3. Place the engine inside the engine mount of your rocket (see Figure 2). The ceramic nozzle needs to be towards the bottom.

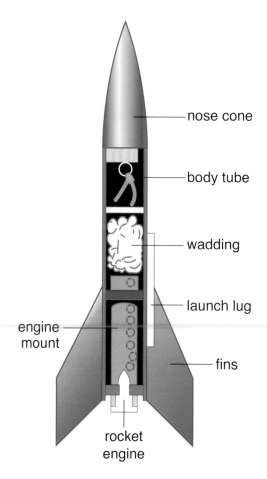

Figure 2

4. Determine the weight of your rocket. Use modeling clay to bring the weight of the rocket up to specifications your teacher gives you. Record the weight of your rocket on the data table. Record the weights of rockets prepared by other laboratory groups on the data table. Extend the data table as needed to accommodate all of the groups in your class.

5. Place the igniter in the bottom of the engine. Slightly bend the wires, making sure that they do not touch each other. Secure the wires to the rocket engine with a piece of masking tape.

6. Set up the launcher in a flat, outdoor area. Make sure that the launcher is stable and will not tip over.

7. When you are ready to launch your rocket, slide the launch lug of your rocket onto the pole of the launcher. Attach the wires of the igniter to the clips of the launcher. The safety system of the launcher must be in place before you attach the clips to the igniter.

8. Set your rocket on the launch pad so that the rocket will launch straight up. Make sure that no one is standing close to the launch site. Count down and press the ignition button. Use the stopwatch to time the duration of the rocket's flight. Record the flight time on the data table in seconds (sec).

9. Collect data from other lab groups on the duration of their flights and add the information to the data table. Analyze the data to determine whether there is a relationship between weight of the rocket and duration of flight.

Data Table		
Number or letter of rocket	**Weight of rocket**	**Duration of flight (sec)**

Analysis

1. Why is the alignment of the fins on the rocket important?
2. Why is a launch lug needed?
3. Why is it important for the wires not to touch?
4. Why do you think rocket engines are used for space travel instead of jet engines?
5. Based on your experimental findings, how does the weight of a rocket affect the duration of its flight?
6. Suggest another experiment you could carry out using rockets.

What's Going On?

The forces acting on a rocket include thrust, weight, and *drag*. Drag is the force that slows a moving object. The weight of a rocket varies depending on its size, construction, and the amount of fuel it carries. Weight is a complex variable in rocketry because fuel is extremely heavy. As soon as the vehicle is launched, it begins burning fuel, reducing its weight. As a result, the weight of fuel is constantly changing. However, in model rockets, fuel weight is a minor factor. The weight of a model rocket is primarily determined by its construction and payload.

Rockets are similar to jets (the types of engines found in large airplanes) in that both are classified as *reaction engines* that rely on gases under pressure to generate thrust. In both cases, pressurized gas is forced out of the end of the vehicles as exhaust, pushing the vehicle forward. However, rockets and jets have some significant differences. Jets carry fuel and rely on oxygen in the air to act as the *oxidizer*. Since there is no oxygen in space, rockets carry fuel and an oxidizer. Both types of chemicals, the fuel and oxidizer, known collectively as the propellants, are very heavy. Propellants make up about 90 percent of a rocket's weight. Once a rocket is launched, propellants burn very quickly. For example, the rocket *Saturn 5*, which carried humans to the Moon for NASA's Apollo missions, consumed 560,000 gallons (gal)(2, 120,000 liter [L]) of propellants in less then 3 minutes (min) of flight.

Connections

The use of rockets as weapons has a long history. The national anthem by author and lawyer Francis Scott Key (1779–1843) includes the line "the rockets red glare," a reference to incendiary rockets used in the War of 1812. These weapons, which were developed by British army officer Sir William Congreve (1772–1828), burned black powder in an iron case. A guide stick was used to stabilize the devices. Another British inventor, William Hale (1797–1870), built a similar rocket that did not require the guide stick. Hales rockets were used by the U.S. Army in the Mexican-American War of 1846–48 and to some extent in the Civil War.

 Want to Know More?

See appendix for Our Findings.

Further Reading

Brain, Marshall. "How Rocket Engines Work," How Stuff Works, 2009. Available online. URL: http://www.howstuffworks.com/rocket.htm. Accessed June 3, 2009. Brain explains thrust, propellants, and drag as well as the differences in liquid and solid fuel rockets.

Glenn Learning Technologies Project. "Forces on a Model Rocket," Rockets for Schools. Available online. URL: http://www.rockets4schools. org/education/Rocket_Forces.pdf. Accessed June 2, 2009. The concepts of thrust, drag, velocity, and acceleration of model rockets are explained in this article.

Heister, Stephen. "Rocket," World Book at NASA, November 29, 2007. Available online. URL: http://www.nasa.gov/worldbook/rocket_worldbook. html. Accessed June 2, 2009. Heister explains solid fuel, liquid fuel, and hybrid rockets, and gives examples of each type.

18. Measuring the Altitude and Speed of a Model Rocket

Topic

The altitude and speed of a model rocket can be determined experimentally.

Introduction

When you launch a model rocket, it shoots high into the sky before falling back to Earth. The launch and flight last only a few minutes. In that short time frame, it is difficult to visualize how high or how fast the rocket traveled. To find out, you must take some measurements during the rocket's flight.

Inclinometers are instruments that measure the angle of slope of objects. The angle can then be used to calculate the height of the object. Astronomers take measurements with inclinometers to find the distance of objects from Earth. However, the instrument is not just for astronomers. Foresters rely on inclinometers to find the height of a natural rock formation, the grade of a slope, or the height of a tree. Meteorologists use them to determine the height of clouds. Civil engineers and builders make use of them to help them determine safe grades. Some skiers even carry inclinometers with them to measure the grade of a ski slope because very steep slopes are prone to dangerous *avalanches*. In this experiment, you will make a simple inclinometer and use it to calculate the height of a rocket's flight. You will also determine the velocity of the rocket.

Time Required

55 minutes

Materials

- access to an outdoor area
- about 12 inches (in.)(30 centimeters [cm]) of heavy-duty black thread

- calculator
- fishing sinker or other light weight that can be tied to the string
- drinking straw with a large diameter
- protractor
- model rocket, assembled and ready to use
- model rocket launcher
- stopwatch
- tape measure
- science notebook

Safety Note Only launch rockets outdoors in an open area on a day when there is little or no wind. Do not launch rockets near dead grass or other flammable vegetation. Stand at least 15 feet (ft) (4.6 meters [m]) away from the rocket when launching. Only use the electrical launching devices that come with the rockets; do not use fuses or matches. Make sure that the igniter's safety key is removed when connecting wires and clips. Make sure that the launch pad is stable so that it will not turn over during launch. Adult supervision is required. Please review and follow the safety guidelines at the beginning of this volume.

Procedure

1. Work with a partner. To make an inclinometer:
   a. Tape the drinking straw to the straight edge of the protractor, being careful not to crush the straw. Tape the straw on the side that is opposite the numbers. The straw acts as an eyepiece (Figure 1).
   b. Tape the black thread to the hole in the protractor, forming a plumb line.
   c. Tie the fishing sinker to the free end of the thread.
2. Set the model rocket on the launcher.
3. Have your partner hold the inclinometer and stand 328 ft (100 m) from the launching site, while you stand at the launching position with the stopwatch and the ignition button.

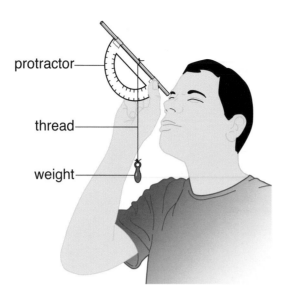

protractor

thread

weight

Figure 1

4. Launch the rocket and start the stopwatch simultaneously.

5. As the rocket ascends, your partner sights it through the eyepiece (straw) of the inclinometer.

6. At the highest point in the rocket's ascent, your partner calls out "Now!" and squeezes the plumb line up against to the protractor to hold its position. At the same time, you stop the stopwatch.

7. You record the time on the stopwatch in your science notebook.

8. Your lab partner reads the angle between the eyepiece and the string and records the angle of the rocket in your science notebook.

9. Determine the altitude of the rocket. To do so:

    a. Subtract the angle recorded in step 8 from 90 degrees to determine angle theta (θ):

        $\theta = 90° -$ your reading

    b. Look up the tangent (tan) of the angle on the data table.

    c. Multiply the tan of angle θ by the distance that your lab partner stood from the launching site (328 ft [100 m]) to find the altitude.

        Altitude = 100mtanθ

    d. To find the total altitude, you must factor in the height of your lab partner using the following formula:

        Total altitude = 100mtanθ + height of your lab partner

Data Table

Angle	Tan	Angle	Tan	Angle	Tan
0	.0000	31	.6009	61	1.8040
1	.0175	32	.6249	62	1.8807
2	.0349	33	.6494	63	1.9626
3	.0524	34	.6745	64	2.0503
4	.0699	35	.7002	65	2.1445
5	.0875	36	.7265	66	2.2460
6	.1051	37	.7536	67	2.359
7	.1228	38	.7813	68	2.4751
8	.1405	39	.8098	69	2.6051
9	.1584	40	.8391	70	2.7475
10	.1763	41	.8693	71	2.9042
11	.1944	42	.9004	72	3.0777
12	.2126	43	.9325	73	3.2709
13	.2309	44	.9657	74	3.4874
14	.2493	45	1.0000	75	3.7321
15	.2679	46	1.0355	76	4.0108
16	.2867	47	1.0724	77	4.3315
17	.3057	48	1.1106	78	4.7046
18	.3249	49	1.1504	79	5.1446
19	.3443	50	1.1918	80	5.6713
20	.3640	51	1.2349	81	6.3138
21	.3839	52	1.2799	82	7.1154
22	.4040	53	1.3270	83	8.1443
23	.4245	54	1.3764	84	9.5144
24	.4452	55	1.4281	85	11.4301
25	.4663	56	1.4826	86	14.3007
26	.4877	57	1.5399	87	19.0811
27	.5095	58	1.6003	88	28.6363
28	.5317	59	1.6643	89	57.2900
29	.5543	60	1.7321	90	—
30	.5774	—	—	—	—

Analysis

1. Determine the speed of the rocket using the following formula:

$$\text{speed} = \frac{\text{total altitude}}{\text{length of flight (seconds [sec])}}$$

2. List at least two factors that determine how high your rocket can reach.

3. What would happen if the thrust of the engine were equal to the weight of the rocket?

4. Is the speed that you calculated the average speed or the maximum speed of the rocket? Explain your answer.

5. Why is the distance that your partner stands from the launching site included in the equation for the altitude?

What's Going On?

Inclinometers are used to measure heights that are not easily measured directly. Tall trees, flagpoles, and model rocket flights are just a few of the objects for which altitudes are difficult to determine. If several people measure the height or altitude of the same object with an inclinometer, they may get slightly different readings. This type of variation is normal if it falls within a range of 5 to 10 degrees. Readings from several individuals can be averaged to find the best data for your calculations.

If you were to graph the height of your rocket flight, it might look something like Figure 2. In this figure, the X-axis represents eye level and the Y-axis the height of the rocket. The inclinometer, shown in the bottom left-hand corner, shows the angle between eye level and the height of the rocket. If you know the distance to the object, you can use this graph to find the rocket's altitude.

Connections

With the help of the star Polaris, the North Star, inclinometers can be used to determine your latitude. Polaris is located almost directly above the north pole. As the Earth spins on its axis below the stars, most stars seem to travel a slow, circular path above our heads. But Polaris, being directly over us, remains fixed. For that reason, Polaris makes a good reference point. When you locate Polaris in the night sky, you know which direction is north. If you measure the angle of Polaris above the horizon, you know your latitude.

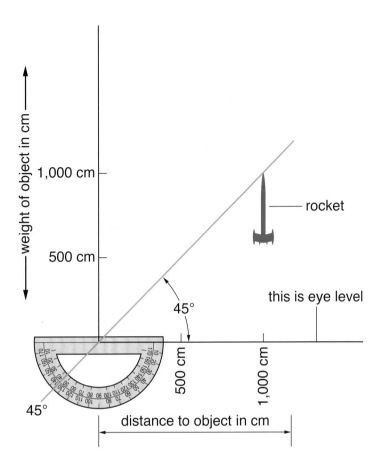

Figure 2

To find Polaris, locate the Big Dipper, a constellation that looks like a cup with a long handle. Find the two stars that make up the right-hand side of the cup (see Figure 3). The bottom star is Merak and the upper one is Dubhe. Draw an imaginary line from these stars straight out into space. The line will intercept a large star; this is Polaris. You can confirm your finding by looking to the right of Polaris for the constellation Cassiopeia, which looks like a flattened "W."

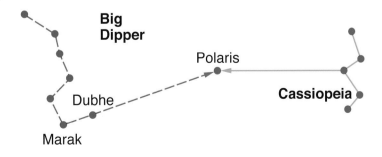

Figure 3

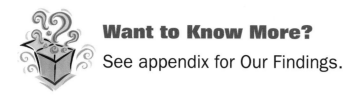

Want to Know More?

See appendix for Our Findings.

Further Reading

Lunar and Planetary Institute. "About Polaris," May 21, 2007. Available online. URL: http://www.lpi.usra.edu/education/skytellers/polaris/about.shtml. Accessed June 4, 2009. This Web page shows how to locate Polaris and explains its importance in navigation.

Minnesota Project Learning Tree. "How to Use a Clinometer." Available online. URL: http://files.dnr.state.mn.us/education_safety/education/plt/activity_sheets/howToUseAClinometer.pdf. Accessed June 4, 2009. Using illustrations, this article explains how an inclinometer helps you find the height of a tree.

Roy, Ken. Science Scope. "Having a blast safely: Model rocketry safety code," November/December 2005. Available online. URL: http://www.coe.tamu.edu/~rcapraro/PBL/PBL%20Research/having%20a%20blast%20in%20PBL.pdf. Accessed June 4, 2009. On this Web page, Roy discusses some of the finer points of safety when using model rockets.

19. Building a Cross-Staff

Topic

A cross-staff like those used by early astronomers can be constructed from materials in the home or laboratory.

Introduction

Before GPS (Global Positioning Systems), scientists relied on some fairly simple devices to determine locations. One instrument, the cross-staff, or Jacob's staff, was used by early astronomers and navigators. Astronomers relied on it to measure the angular distance between two stars, which could be useful in determining stellar location. Navigators found their *latitudes* with the cross-staff. Latitude could be determined by comparing one's position on Earth to either the Sun or Polaris, the north star.

A cross-staff is made of a long staff or piece of wood with a crosspiece that slides back and forth. Mounted on the crosspiece are two sights. To measure the angle between two stars, an astronomer holds the staff just below eye level, then adjusts the crosspiece until a star is centered in each sight. In this activity, you will build a simple cross-staff.

Time Required

45 minutes

Materials

- meterstick
- 12 inch (in.) (30 centimeter [cm]) wooden ruler
- cardboard
- 2 index cards
- scissors
- rubber bands

⚬⬦   stapler

⚬⬦   science notebook

Safety Note   Please review and follow the safety guidelines at the beginning of this volume.

Procedure

1. Make a sleeve on the meterstick with the cardboard and a rubber band. To do so:

    a. cut a strip of cardboard that is about 5 in. (12 cm) by 2 in. (5 cm).

    b. Fold the cardboard so that it wraps completely around the meterstick, forming a sleeve.

    c. Slide the folded cardboard to one end of the meterstick.

    d. Wrap a rubber band around the folded cardboard. The rubber band should fit tightly enough to hold the sleeve together, but not so tightly that the sleeve cannot be shifted along the length of the meterstick. Use 2 more rubber bands to make an "X" on top of the sleeve.

2. Make the crosspiece. To do so, carefully push a ruler beneath the rubber band "X" holding the sleeve so that the ruler is perpendicular to the meterstick. The cross of the "X" should be in the center of the ruler (see Figure 1).

3. Make two smaller sleeves that will fit on each end of the crosspiece. To do so:

    a. Cut two strips of cardboard that measure about 5 in. (12 cm) by 1.2 in. (3 cm).

    b. Fold one piece of cardboard around the right end of the crosspiece and secure it with a rubber band. Use two more rubber bands to make an X on the sleeve.

    c. Repeat step 3b to make a sleeve for the left end of the crosspiece.

4. Make two supports on the tops of the small sleeves. To do so:

    a. Cut two strips from the cardboard about 0.5 in. (1.5 cm) by 4 in. (10 cm).

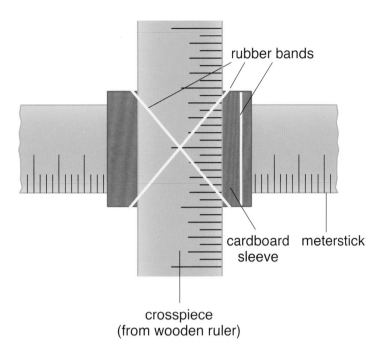

rubber bands

cardboard   meterstick
sleeve

crosspiece
(from wooden ruler)

Figure 1

b. Slide one strip through the "X" on one sleeve so that it is perpendicular to the crosspiece. The middle of the cardboard should be under the "X." Place the other strip on the other sleeve.

c. Crease and bend the strips so that they can each support one of the index cards that you will make in step 5 (see Figure 2).

5. Cut two relatively wide slits in each index card. (See the finished cross-staff in Figure 3). The slits should be about 0.2 in. (4 millimeters [mm]) wide and 1.5 in. (4 cm) long.

6. Insert one index card between the upright parts of one of the supports you made in step 4. When the card is in position, the slits are perpendicular to the crosspiece. Staple the card to the supports. Do the same with the other card and support. (If the supports are too long, trim them with scissors.)

7. The finished cross-staff should resemble Figure 3. Hold the cross-staff so that one end of the meterstick rests on your cheek, just below one eye. Sight down the length of the meterstick. An astronomer would aim the device between two stars, placing one star in each slit.

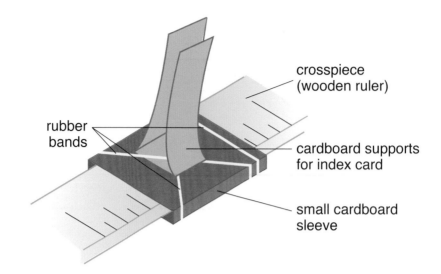

Figure 2

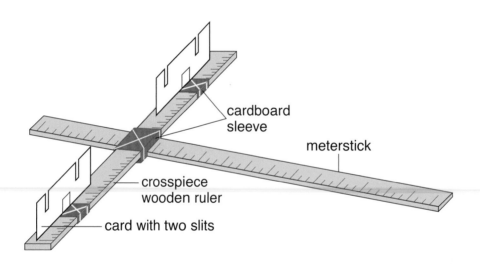

Figure 3

Analysis

1. How did early navigators use a cross-staff?
2. How did early astronomers use a cross-staff?
3. On your cross-staff, what is the purpose of the sleeves?
4. What is the function of the slits in the index cards?
5. Suggest some other uses of a cross-staff.

What's Going On?

A cross-staff makes angular measurements that can be used to find distance. After an astronomer has sighted two stars with the cross-staff, he or she lowers the instrument and measures the distance between his or her eye and the crosspiece and between the center of the cross-staff and the sight. Using simple math, the angular distance can be calculated.

The parts of a cross-staff are relatively simple. The sleeve enables the crosspiece to be moved back and forth so that the observed objects can be sighted through the slits. There are two sets of slits on each index card. If the observed objects are very distant, the inner slits can be used. However, the outer slits are more useful if the objects are relatively close to the observer.

Connections

The first to use a cross-staff may have been Chaldean astronomers around 400 B.C.E. In the 14th century, German mathematician and astronomer Johannes Werner (1468–1522) pointed out that the cross-staff would be a convenient navigational device for sailors. At that time, the instrument was made from a long staff about 36 in. (91 cm) long. Across the staff lay four crosspieces of graduated sizes. The astronomer would hold the staff to his eye and then move a crosspiece back and forth along the staff until it was lined up with the star on top and the horizon on the lower edge. The star's altitude could then be read from a scale on the staff.

 ### Want to Know More?

See appendix for Our Findings.

Further Reading

The Golden Hind. "Golden Hind Education Worksheet—Navigation." Available online. URL: http://www.goldenhind.co.uk/education/ worksheets/navigate.html. Accessed June 10, 2009. Early instruments such as maps, cross-staffs, and astrolabes are pictured and described on this Web page.

Stroebel, Nick. "Stars, What Are They Like?" June 2, 2007. Available online. URL: http://www.astronomynotes.com/starprop/s2.htm. Accessed June 10, 2009. Stroebel explains the usefulness of angular measurements in the study of astronomy.

Willoz-Egnor, Jeanne. The Institute of Navigation, "Cross-staff," Navigation Museum. Available online. URL: http://www.ion.org/museum/item_view. cfm?cid=6&scid=13&iid=26. Accessed June 11, 2009. The use and construction of a navigation cross-staff is discussed on this Web page.

20. The Parallax Effect

Topic

The parallax effect can be used to determine the angular distances between celestial objects.

Introduction

How would you measure the distance between two stars? As you can imagine, such a measurement cannot be made directly. Astronomers use indirect measurements to find remote distances. One method of securing an indirect measurement is by using the *parallax effect*, the apparent displacement of an object because the observer's point of view changes. You have experienced the parallax effect when you ride along the highway and view a distant object from one point, then later from a different point. In Figure 1, an observer is viewing a tree in front of a mountain. The observer's movement makes the apparent position of the tree change. However, you know that the tree has not moved; it just seems to have moved.

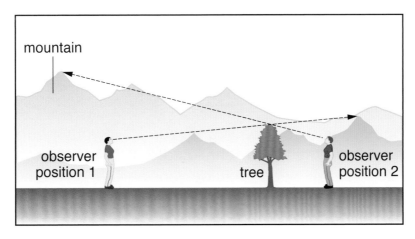

Figure 1

Over time, a star's position in the night sky will seem to change in relation to the background of the distant stars. This apparent change is due to the fact that as the Earth travels through its orbit, it changes positions. Astronomers can use the star's position on two different occasions to determine its location. In this experiment, you will measure distances using the parallax effect.

Time Required

55 minutes

Materials

- ruler
- calculator
- access to an outdoor area at night to observe the night sky
- wall or chalkboard
- cross-staff (commercial or the one made in experiment 19)
- science notebook

Safety Note   Take care when working outdoors. Please review and
follow the safety guidelines at the beginning of this volume.

Procedure, Part A

1. To observe the parallax effect, extend your arm in front of your face and hold up one finger.

2. Position your finger in front of a point on the wall or chalkboard so that your finger covers the point.

3. Close one eye and observe your finger. Have your laboratory partner make a mark on the wall or chalkboard at the point now covered by your finger (you will need to guide your partner to the correct spot).

4. Close the other eye and observe your finger. Have your partner make a mark on the wall or chalkboard at the position now covered by your finger. Measure the distance between the two marks.

5. Answer Analysis questions 1 and 2.

Procedure, Part B

1. Follow your teacher to an outdoor viewing area at night.

2. Give you eyes a few minutes to adjust to the dark.

3. You will use a cross-staff and the parallax effect to determine the angle between two stars. First, determine which two stars you will measure. For example, you might use two bright stars in the Big Dipper.

4. A cross-staff is made of a staff, a crosspiece on a slider, and two cards that contain slits. Slide the crosspiece of a cross-staff to about the middle of the staff. Put the staff up to your cheek and sight it midway between the two stars.

5. Adjust the slider on the crosspiece until the slits on the cards are lined up so that you see one star in each slit (see Figure 2). Notice that there are two slits in each card. You must use either the inner pair of slits or the outer pair of slits.

6. Lower the cross-staff and measure the distance between the slits.

7. To find the angular separation of the stars:

    Find the distance along the ruler between the slits (B to B^1) in centimeters. For example, if one star was sighted at the 10 cm mark and the other at the 15 cm mark, then the angular separation is 5 cm or 5°:

8. Answer the remaining of the Analysis questions.

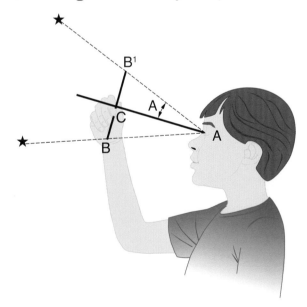

Figure 2

Analysis

1. How did the apparent position of your finger change when you alternated eyes?

2. Your eyes are a few inches apart. How does this explain your observations of the apparent shift in your finger's position?

3. What is the function of a cross-staff?

4. Why might an astronomer want to find the angular separation of stars?

5. When do you think a parallax would be ineffective?

What's Going On?

Angular distance is useful in astronomy. If you find the angle between two stars, you can use the parallax effect to calculate the distance to those stars. First, a star's position against background stars is measured; six months later, the star's position relative to the same background stars is measured again. The change in angular distance over 6 months equals 186 million miles (299 km), the diameter of the orbit of Earth. Figure 3 demonstrates how these measurements can be made.

Calculations of distance to stars are based on *triangulation*, the technique of solving for the sides of a triangle if the angles and length of one side can be measured. In this experiment, the triangle formed between the staff and a star is extremely long and thin. Half the crosspiece served as the base of the triangle. The distance from you to the star you measured is represented by one side of the triangle.

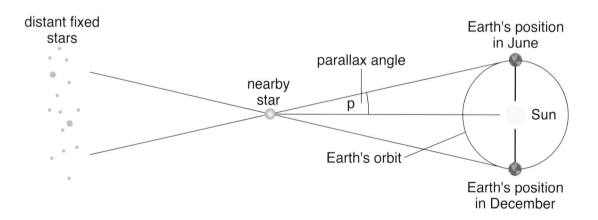

Figure 3

Connections

Stars seem to move in the heavens, but their apparent shift is due to parallax caused by changes in the Earth's position. Stellar parallax is determined by observing a star's position in the sky at different times of year. Although observations and measurements of stars can be made from Earth, the atmosphere and magnetic field interfere with accuracy. The satellite *Hipparcos* (High Precision Parallax Collecting Satellite) was launched in 1989 to overcome these problems. Due to its position, the satellite improved the ability to measure with parallax by tenfold. During its time in space (1989–93), *Hipparcos* collected data on more than 100,000 stars, a tremendous amount of work, but an accomplishment that accounted for less than 1 percent of the total area of our galaxy, the Milky Way. In 2011, the European Space Agency will launch the Gaia mission which will be able to measure stars at even greater distances from Earth.

Want to Know More?

See appendix for Our Findings.

Further Reading

European Organization for Astronomical Study in the Southern Hemisphere. "Astronomy Online." Available online. URL: http://www.eso.org/public/outreach/eduoff/aol/. Accessed June 11, 2009. This Web site discusses a number of topics in astronomy, including parallax.

Knop, Robert. "Measuring Angular Distances," August 18, 2005. Available online. URL: http://brahms.phy.vanderbilt.edu/a103/info/angdist.shtml. Accessed June 11, 2009. Knop explains a method of measuring angular distance with a crossbow on this Web page.

Pogge, Richard. "Lecture 5: Distances of Stars," October 31, 2006. Available online. URL: http://www.astronomy.ohio-state.edu/~pogge/Ast162/Unit1/distances.html. Accessed June 11, 2009. This Web page contains an outline that briefly explains the use of parallax in determining distance.

Scope and Sequence Chart

This chart aligns the experiments in this book with some of the National Science Content Standards. (These experiments do not address every national science standard.) Please refer to your local and state content standards for additional information. As always, adult supervision is recommended and discretion should be used in selecting an experiment appropriate to each age group or to individual students.

Standard	Grades 5–8	Grades 9–12
Physical Science		
Properties and changes of properties in matter		
Chemical reactions	2, 5	2, 5
Motions and forces	13, 14, 17	13, 14, 17
Transfer of energy and interactions of energy and matter	1, 2, 3, 5, 6, 7, 17	1, 2, 3, 5, 6, 7, 17
Conservation of energy and increase in disorder	1	1
Life Science		
Cells and structure and function in living systems		
Reproduction and heredity		
Regulation and behavior		

Standard	Grades 5–8	Grades 9–12
Populations and ecosystems		
Diversity and adaptations of organisms		
Interdependence of organisms		
Matter, energy, and organization in living systems		
Biological evolution		
Earth Science		
Structure and energy in the Earth system	1, 2 , 3, 4, 10, 11, 13, 14, 16	1, 2, 3, 4, 10, 11, 13, 14, 16
Geochemical cycles	6	6
Origin and evolution of the Earth system		
Origin and evolution of the universe	16	16
Earth in the solar system	8, 9, 10, 11, 12, 15, 19, 20	8, 9, 10, 11, 12, 15, 19, 20
Nature of Science		
Science in history	7, 8, 9, 13, 15, 19	7, 8, 9, 13, 15, 19
Science as an endeavor	all	all

Grade Level

Setting

The experiments are classified by materials and equipment use as follows:

- Those under SCHOOL LABORATORY involve materials and equipment found only in science laboratories. Those under SCHOOL LABORATORY must be carried out there under the supervision of the teacher or author adult.

- Those under HOME involve household or everyday materials. Some of these can be done at home, but call for supervision.

- The experiments classified under OUTDOORS may be done at the school or at the home, but call for supervision.

SCHOOL LABORATORY

HOME

OUTDOORS

OUTDOORS

Our Findings

1. VISIBLE AND INFRARED LIGHT

Idea for class discussion: Find out what students already know about electromagnetic radiation by asking them to describe some of the characteristics of sunlight.

Analysis

1. Visible light has wavelengths between 3.8×10^7 and 7.6×10^7 nm and frequencies between 3.9×10^{14} -and 7.9×10^{14} nm. Infrared light has wavelengths between 7.6×10^7 and 0.001 nm and frequencies between 3×10^{11} and 3.9×10^{14} nm.

2. The wavelength of an electromagnetic wave is the distance between crests. The frequency of a wave is the number of crests that pass a fixed point within a given time. When crests are closer together, waves will have a higher frequency, and a higher frequency wave carries a greater amount of energy.

3. Gamma rays carry the most energy of all electromagnetic waves.

4. Light filters are made of special materials that block specific wavelengths of electromagnetic radiation but let all others pass through. Light filters vary in color and material type depending on the wavelengths that they are able to block.

5. Visible light can be seen with the naked eye, it does not carry any heat, and it can be broken up into different colors depending on the wavelength of the light. Infrared radiation cannot be seen with the naked eye, it has a longer wavelength than visible light, and it carries heat energy.

6. Answers will vary. Infrared light is given off when heat is released. Therefore, infrared light can be detected and interpreted using a thermogenic scanner to detect heat leaks within homes and businesses, and it is used in night vision goggles. Infrared radiation can also be used to detect objects in space that do not give off enough energy to be detected within the visible spectrum.

2. CORONAL EJECTIONS

Idea for class discussion: Show students photographs or a short video of the northern lights. Explain that materials from the Sun's surface can be spewed into space and that these materials contain charged particles that are responsible for the northern lights as well as other phenomena.

Analysis

1. Answers will vary based on the images chosen by students. The average velocity should be around 700 to 950 km/s.

2. Answers will vary but will range from about 45 to about 50 hours.

3. Answers will vary based on the images chosen by students. The acceleration will probably be a negative number.

4. Answers will vary based on the images chosen by students; most likely, student answers will reflect that the mass ejection is slowing down.

3. SPEED OF ELECTROMAGNETIC ENERGY

Idea for class discussion: Ask students why we can see the planets in the night sky or with telescopes. Point out that we can only see objects that emit light or send reflected light to our eyes. Light is one type of electromagnetic radiation.

Notes to the teacher: Part A must be done outdoors. The entire scale of Part A requires about 1/2 mile (0.8 km). To accommodate this, have students who represent the planets form a long wavy line rather than a straight one. Even if you do not have enough space to show all of the planets, you might be able to represent some of them and so get across the idea of the size of the orbits and the distances between the planets.

Analysis

1. 1,019 paces

2. larger

3. Uranus is at the halfway point.

4. Student predictions will vary. Answers will reflect student opinions.

5. No. The Earth and all of the other planets are constantly in motion. Planets move on different paths at different velocities and sometimes move closer to each other than at other times.

6. Answers may vary. Because of its orbit, Pluto's distance from the Sun varies. Light from the Sun can take from 4.1 to 6.8 hours to reach Pluto.

7. Yes. The Sun does not move, but the Earth does. The distance between Earth and other planets is constantly changing. Although the distance between the Sun and each planet varies during the orbit of the planet, the distance does not change as much as it would between two planets orbiting on different planes.

8. Answers will vary based on student opinions. Electromagnetic radiation always travels at the same speed although the waves may have different wavelengths and frequencies.

4. SATURN'S RINGS

Idea for class discussion: Find out what students already know about the composition of Saturn's rings. Write their ideas on the board and reexamine them after the experiment.

Analysis

1. Saturn is made of mostly hydrogen, helium, and some other trace elements.

2. From the most internal to most external: D Ring, C Ring, Columbo Gap, Maxwell Gap, B Ring, Cassini Division, Huygens Gap, A Ring, Encke Division, Keeler Gap, Roche Division, F Ring, G Ring, E Ring.

3. Saturn's rings are made of dense clouds containing solid chunks of ice ranging from microscopic to massive (house-sized) and debris.

4. Saturn's rings are held in place by its gravitational and magnetic field.

5. Saturn is not a true sphere. Because of the speed of Saturn's rotation, the planet is flattened at the poles and bulges slightly near the equator.

6. A day on Saturn is approximately 10 1/2 hours long.

7. Saturn has 60 moons that have been discovered and named. However, answers may vary because this number changes as discoveries are made.

5. HOW EFFICIENT IS A SOLAR PANEL?

Idea for class discussion: Ask students to make a list of the sources of power that we rely on to provide us with electricity. Discuss some of the advantages and disadvantages of those that involve coal and oil.

Analysis

1. Answers will vary based on student results.

2. Amperage is the flow of current. Voltage is the difference in electric potential between two regions. Power, or wattage, is the rate of energy transfer.

3. Answers will vary based on student results. Student answers will most likely be between 10 and 18 percent.

4. Answers will vary based on student results.

5. Answers will vary. Some benefits may include: Solar energy is cost-efficient if you live in a sunny region. Additionally, it does not have the waste or dangerous by-products that many of the fossil fuel–based energy sources contain. Some disadvantages include: the initial cost of equipment and that it is only useful when there is sunshine.

6. Answers will vary. Some suggested answers include having more silicon panels, covering the panel with antireflective material, and filtering out the radiation that causes the panel to overheat.

6. KINETIC ENERGY OF IMPACT

Idea for class discussion: Discuss with students the difference in kinetic and potential energy. Ask students to give examples of each.

Analysis

1. Answers will vary. Possible answers include, mass, velocity, and diameter.

2. Answers will vary. Students should choose the ball that they think would create the largest crater.

3. Answers will vary based on the balls used and their sizes.

4. Answers will vary based on student data.

5. Answers will vary based on student data.

6. Student graphs will vary, but all should include labeled axes with the crater size on the Y-axis and kinetic energy on the X-axis.

7. The balls with greater kinetic energy produced larger craters. This is because they hit the ground with more force and caused the sand to shift more than the smaller balls with less mass and kinetic energy. Thus the relationship is positive—the greater the energy level the larger the crater.

8. Answers will vary. Kinetic energy increases with more freefall time. Therefore, if the balls were dropped from a lower height, there would be less kinetic energy and there would be more kinetic energy if the balls were dropped from a higher location.

7. A SIMPLE SPECTROSCOPE TO IDENTIFY GASES

Idea for class discussion: Engage students in a discussion on the colors of stars. If possible, show them pictures of stars of different colors. Help them understand that the light produced by stars has special characteristics based on temperature, speed of the star, and the star's composition.

Notes to the teacher: For this experiment, collect CDs or DVDs that are not needed for other purposes. Spectrum tubes of various gases (such as argon, chlorine, hydrogen, mercury, and neon) and a spectrum tube power supply are available from scientific supply companies. Reveal the names of the "known" gases to students. Conceal names of gases that you want to use as "unknowns."

Analysis

1. A spectroscope can inform astronomers about the temperature, age, and history of individual stars.

2. When an atom gets excited, its electrons move to a higher energy level; as the electrons return to their original state, they give off light. Each element has its own unique colors that are given off.

3. The colors faded into each other.

4. Answer will vary depending on which light sources (known gases) were used, but should include the colors that were seen.

5. Light from distant stars and galaxies have very similar spectra, which lets astronomers know that hydrogen is the main component of the stars. They can tell this because the spectra are similar.

8. VIEWING JUPITER THROUGH A SIMPLE TELESCOPE

Idea for class discussion: Discuss the relative positions and sizes of Earth and Jupiter. Ask students how they envision the surface of Jupiter.

Notes to the teacher: View Jupiter in a location as far as possible from city lights.

Analysis

1. Pictures will vary based on student observations.

2. Pictures will vary based on student observations. This picture should be more clear and detailed than the previous one.

3. Answers will vary. The image through the simple homemade telescope should be upside down compared to the commercial one, since there are no reflecting mirrors inside of the homemade one. Additionally, the commercial telescope image was most likely much more clear and detailed than the simple one.

4. Since Jupiter rotates approximately once every 10 hours, to see Jupiter's opposite side through a telescope you would have to look at it in the early morning hours tomorrow, 10 hours after viewing it tonight, or wait until two nights from now and view Jupiter 2 hours later than the time it was viewed tonight.

9. SUNSPOT MONITOR

Idea for class discussion: Ask students the chemical makeup of the Sun. The orb is made of approximately 75 percent hydrogen and 25 percent helium. The Sun's energy comes from nuclear reactions at the core.

Analysis

1. Sunspots are caused by increased levels of magnetic activity within the Sun.

2. Graphs will vary. The number of sunspots should be on the Y-axis and the days should be across the X-axis. All parts of the graph should be labeled and lines should connect the plotted points.

3. Answers will vary based on student results.

4. Answers will vary based on student results.

5. Answers will vary based on student results. Generally, sunspots are found closer to the poles when there are few sunspots and closer to the equator during a peak year.

10. HOW DOES LIGHT INTENSITY VARY WITH DISTANCE?

Idea for class discussion: Discuss with students some of the basics of designing a reliable experiment including controls and variables.

Analysis

1. Answers will vary based on student procedures. Answers may include descriptions of measurements at set distances, covering the setup with a box to avoid any additional light from entering, or using the same measuring techniques for all parts of the experiment.

2. Answers will vary. Scientific experiments are developed to test one specific factor, known as the experimental factor. To truly determine if that one factor is having an effect, all other parts of the test must remain constant.

3. Graphs will vary based on student results. Graphs should include the distance on the X-axis, light intensity on the Y-axis, and plots connected to make an L-shaped arc.

4. Answers will vary based on student procedure.

5. Answers will vary based on student results.

6. Factors influencing temperatures on planets include the atmosphere and how much heat is retained, the composition of the planet (gaseous or terrestrial), planetary topography, and distance from the Sun.

11. FLASHLIGHT MAGNITUDE

Idea for class discussion: Ask students to imagine that they are driving at night and see two sets of headlights: One set of headlights is much brighter than the other. With this little bit of information, ask students which vehicle would they expect to be closer to them. Most will say the one with brighter headlights. Point out how this might not be true.

The dimmer headlights might be very close, but very low on power. Use this thinking to introduce the idea of magnitude of light in the sky.

Analysis

1. Answers will vary. The largest flash light probably gives off the most light.

2. The closer the light is to the wall, the brighter it appears to be.

3. Scientists need to be able to tell which stars are truly brightest as well as which stars look brightest to people on Earth.

4. Student answers may vary. Students would have to assign the bright light a negative value.

5. Stars are more visible in areas with low amounts of artificial light. Light pollution greatly reduces the visibility of stars. Many more stars are visible in areas with low or no light pollution.

12. HOW LONG IS TWILIGHT?

Idea for class discussion: Have students write their own descriptions of twilight. Share two or three with the class.

Analysis

1. Answers will vary depending on student's location.

2. Answers will vary.

3. Graphs will vary. Students should have months listed along the X-axis and the length of twilight (in hours) on the Y-axis, with bars depicting the average day length for each month.

4. The longest twilight hours are generally in the summer (usually June) and winter near the solstices. The shortest are close to the spring and fall equinoxes. Seasonal variation is minimal near the equator.

5. Twilight is longer near the poles than at the equator.

13. ACCELERATION DUE TO GRAVITY

Idea for class discussion: Drop a large and a small ball simultaneously and ask students whether they hit the floor at the same time. Have them explain their reasoning.

Analysis

1. Yes, because gravity acts on all objects in the same manner.

2. Answers will vary.

3. The closer you come to starting and stopping the stop watch at the correct times, the more accurate your results will be.

4. The wadded paper hits the ground first.

5. The sheet that is not wadded has more air resistance.

14. THE LAW OF INERTIA

Idea for class discussion: Ask students which seems to be true: An object in motion will remain in motion until stopped, or a stationary object will remain stationary until set in motion. Have them explain their reasoning.

Analysis

1. Student answers will vary.

2. Student answers will vary but should include an explanation of reasoning.

3. Student answers will vary. The ball should achieve a height almost equal to its starting height.

4. The addition of lubricant increases the height which the ball can achieve.

5. Student answers will vary. Friction prevents the ball from reaching the starting height.

15. WHO KNOWS TEN CONSTELLATIONS?

Idea for class discussion: Ask a few students to name and describe their favorite constellations.

Analysis

1. A small group will not reflect the thinking of the entire school.

2. Students answers will vary depending on survey results.

3. Students answers will vary depending on survey results.

4. Students answers will vary depending on survey results.

5. Students answers will vary depending on survey results.

16. THE SIZE OF THE UNIVERSE

Idea for class discussion: Ask students which is closer to us, the center of our galaxy or the nearest star. (The nearest star is closer to Earth.) Students have trouble visualizing distances in space because they are so vast. Explain that this investigation will help them appreciate these distances.

Analysis

1. Answers will vary depending on the scales students use.

2. The Moon is too close to Earth to be included on this scale.

3. Light from the star left that star 10 years ago. We cannot see that star's present.

4. 93 million miles (150 million km)

5. No. We can only see objects because of the light they produce or reflect.

17. ROCKET SCIENCE

Idea for class discussion: Review Newton's three laws of motion. Point out that all three laws are applicable to the motion of rockets.

Notes to the teacher: Model rocket kits and rocket launchers are available at hobby stores or toy stores. Rocket engine size is specified in the kit instructions. In this experiment, students are comparing the effect of weight on duration of flight. Assign each lab group a weight. For example, if the assembled rockets weigh 50 grams (g), you might assign one group a weight of 53 g, another group a weight of 56 g, and so forth. Do not launch rockets on windy days.

Analysis

1. The fins help direct and guide the rocket.

2. The launch lug helps the rocket to go up in the air and keeps it from tipping over when it is first ignited.

3. If the wires were to touch then they would "short out" and the rocket would not launch.

4. Rocket engines are used because rockets carry the substances used for thrust in them. Jet engines use air for thrust; since there is no air in space, a jet engine would be worthless.

5. Answers will vary depending on experimental findings.

6. Answers will vary. Students might suggest finding out how the shape of a rocket's fins effects flight duration.

18. MEASURING THE ALTITUDE AND SPEED OF A MODEL ROCKET

Idea for class discussion: Ask students how they might measure the height of a model rocket's flight. Students might suggest comparing the height to a nearby tree or building. Explain that this experiment will give them a more accurate measurement.

Analysis

1. Answers will vary.

2. Factors vary but could include size of the engine, size of the rocket, and wind.

3. The rocket would not move.

4. It is the average speed.

5. It is included because the distance that you stand from an object affects the angle at which you view that object.

19. BUILDING A CROSS-STAFF

Idea for class discussion: Ask students to list some uses of a GPS device. Ask them how they think people who lived hundreds of years ago found locations.

Analysis

1. Navigators used it to determine latitude.

2. Astronomers used it to find the angular distance between two stars.

3. The sleeves move the crosspiece forward and back.

4. The slits serve as sights.

5. Answers will vary but might include surveying.

20. THE PARALLAX EFFECT

Idea for class discussion: Ask students how they might measure the distance to a distant building or tree if they did not have a tape measure. Lead them to understand that some measurements can be made indirectly.

Analysis

1. The finger seemed to move from side to side.

2. Even though they are only a few inches apart, the eyes have different perspectives.

3. A cross-staff is the instrument used to measure angular distance between two remote objects.

4. Angular separation can be used to calculate the distance from Earth to objects in space.

5. Answers will vary. When it is so small that you cannot see a change from one eye to the other.

Glossary

acceleration increase in rate of change of velocity

alternating current electric current in which the direction of electron flow reverses in regular cycles

angular distance angular separation of two objects as perceived by an observer

apparent magnitude measure of the brightness of a celestial object viewed from Earth

asteroid small celestial object, larger than a meteorite but smaller than a planet, that orbits the Earth

astronaut person trained for space flight

astronomical twilight span of time beginning in the morning and ending in the evening when the Sun is 18 degrees below the horizon

avalanche large slide of snow, rock, and ice along a slope

candela basic unit of luminous intensity, equal to 12.5 lumens

civil twilight span of time beginning in the morning and ending in the evening when the Sun is 6 degrees below the horizon

coma cloud of gases and dust surrounding the frozen nucleus of a comet

comet frozen mass of particles that orbits the Sun on a highly elliptical path

constellation pattern of stars as viewed from Earth

corona luminous atmosphere of ionized gases outside the chromosphere of the Sun

coronal mass ejections explosion of hot plasma from the Sun's surface

coronograph telescope attachment that blocks the Sun's direct light, making it possible to photograph the corona

crespular referring to the time of day when light levels are low

diffract to bend a wave around an obstacle or through a small opening

diffraction grating optical device with numerous parallel grooves that splits light into its wavelengths creating spectra

direct current electric current in which electrons flow in one direction only

Doppler effect change in the apparent wavelength of a wave as perceived by an observer moving toward or away from the source of the wave

drag resistance to motion through a fluid

ejecta material that is ejected when an impact crater forms

electromagnetic radiation energy that travels in a wave and has both magnetic and electrical characteristics

electromagnetic spectrum the entire range of frequencies of electromagnetic waves

elliptical path oval path followed by some objects in orbit

energy the ability to do work

frequency number of waves that pass a point in a given period of time

friction force that resists the motion of an object

gravitational constant gravitational force between two objects that is directly proportional to the mass of the objects and inversely proportional to the distance between them

heliosphere region in space around the Sun that is influenced by solar wind and the solar magnetic field

illuminance amount of light falling on a surface divided by the area of the surface

impact crater crater formed from the impact of an object such as a meteorite

inclinometer device used to measure the angle of a line of sight above the horizon

inertia the tendency of a body to maintain its state of rest or motion until acted upon by some outside force

infrared radiation electromagnetic energy with wavelengths longer than visible light but shorter than radio waves

kinetic energy the energy of a body due to its motion

latitude measure, in degrees, of relative positions north or south on the Earth's surface, shown on maps and globes by lines that are parallel to the equator

light pollution excessive light created by humans, especially around cities, that interferes with the visibility of stars and other celestial bodies

lumen measure of the perceived intensity of light

luminance measurement of luminous intensity in one direction

lux measurement of illuminance equal to one lumen per square meter

magnitude measure of brightness of a star

meteorite small, natural stony or metallic object from space that reaches Earth's surface

meteoroid small, natural stony or metallic object in space that orbits the Sun

nanometer unit of length equal to one billionth of a meter

nautical twilight span of time beginning in the morning and ending in the evening when the Sun is 12 degrees below the horizon

northern lights display of lights and colors in the atmosphere caused by ionized particles from the Sun; also known as the aurora borealis

oxidizer chemical that aids in the combustion of fuel

parallax effect apparent change in the position of an object due to a change in position of the observer

payload goods carried by a rocket, including munitions and cargo

penumbra region of shadow near the darkest region of a sunspot

photon an elementary particle and the basic unit of electromagnetic radiation

photovoltaic cell device that converts the Sun's energy into electricity; also called a solar cell

plasma fourth state of matter found in stars that is created when a gas is superheated and loses it electrons, becoming a cloud of nuclei and free electrons

potential energy energy that can be converted into other forms, such as kinetic energy

pyranometer device that measures the amount of light reaching Earth's surface

reaction engine engine that propels a vehicle forward by expelling burning gases

shooting star path of light produced by a meteorite burning in the Earth's atmosphere

solar flare   eruption of solar gases from the Sun's surface

solar panel   electrical device made up of a group of interconnected photovoltaic cells

spectrometer   optical instrument used to analyze energy in the electromagnetic spectrum

spectroscope   optical instrument used to separate light into its component colors for analysis

sunspot   dark spot on the Sun that is cooler than the surrounding solar surface

thrust   reaction force produced when a system expels mass in one direction producing a proportional but opposite force that moves a vehicle forward

triangulation   method of locating an unknown point by using a triangle in which the unknown point and two known points are the corners

ultraviolet radiation   electromagnetic energy with wavelengths shorter than visible light but longer than X-rays

umbra   darkest region of a sunspot

velocity   the speed at which an object is moving

volt   unit of electrical potential or pressure

wavelength   distance from the peak of one wave to the peak of the next wave

zodiac   band of the sky that is divided into twelve regions, each defined by a constellation

Internet Resources

The World Wide Web is an invaluable source of information for students, teachers, and parents. The following list is intended to help you get started exploring educational sites that relate to the book. It is just a sample of the Web material that is available to you. All of these sites were accessible as of June 2009.

Educational Resources

American Chemical Society. "Periodic Table of the Elements." Available online. URL: http://acswebcontent.acs.org/games/pt.html. Accessed March 5, 2009. This interactive Web page is devoted to the Periodic Table and offers up-to-date information on its elements and electron configurations.

Astronomy.com. Kalmbach Publishing Company, 2009. Available online. URL: http://www.astronomy.com/asy/default.aspx. Accessed June 11, 2009. This online magazine provides news, images of the sky each month, an interactive star atlas, and other resources.

Astronomy Now Online. Pole Star Publications, 2006. Available online. URL: http://www.astronomynow.com/. Accessed June 11, 2009. This Web site of a United Kingdom magazine provides articles on a range of topics related to astronomy.

BBC. "Science and Nature: Space." Available online. URL: http://www.bbc.co.uk/science/space/deepspace/index.shtml. Accessed May 29, 2009. Links to information on black holes, dark matter, worm holes, and other topics are provided on this Web site.

Caltech Astronomy. "The Big Picture." Available online. URL: http://bigpicture.caltech.edu/. Accessed May 27, 2009. The Big Picture is a digital sky image taken from the center of the Virgo Cluster.

Cool Cosmo. "Infrared Astronomy." Available online. URL: http://coolcosmos.ipac.caltech.edu/cosmic_classroom/ir_tutorial/importance.html. Accessed March 15, 2009. This NASA Web site explains how astronomers use infrared radiation to study the universe.

Guidry, Mike. "Violence in the Cosmos: Explosive Processes and the Evolution of the Universe." Available online. URL: http://csep10.phys.utk.edu/guidry/violence/violence-root.html. Accessed May 29, 2009. Guidry explains how the explosions that produced stars and galaxies are responsible for the universe as we know it in this online article.

Jet Propulsion Laboratory. "Cassini Equinox Mission." Available online. URL: http://saturn.jpl.nasa.gov/index.cfm. Accessed May 27, 2009. Stories and photographs about Cassini, a space probe to Saturn, are provided on this NASA Web page.

Kids Know It Network. "Kidsastronomy.com," 2009. Available online. URL: http://www.kidsastronomy.com/. Accessed May 27, 2009. On this Web site, students can view animations of the solar system and objects in deep space.

Learn What's Up. "Starcharts." Available online. URL; http://www.learnwhatsup.com/astro/index1.shtml. Accessed May 27, 2009. By clicking on links on this Web site, one can access star charts for specific months and locations.

Lousteaux, Lydia. "*Astronomy Today*'s Skyguide," *Astronomy Today*, 2009. Available online. URL: http://www.astronomytoday.com/skyguide.html. Accessed May 27, 2009. By accessing this Web page, one can find out which planets, stars, constellations, meteor showers, and other sights are available in the night sky.

Michigan Technological University. "The Aurora Page, 2008." Available online. URL: http://www.geo.mtu.edu/weather/aurora/. Accessed May 27, 2009. Beautiful photographs and interesting explanations of the aurora borealis are provided on this Web site.

National Maritime Museum. "The Universe," January 4, 2005. Available online. URL: http://www.nmm.ac.uk/explore/astronomy-and-time/astronomy-facts/universe/galaxies. Accessed May 29, 2009. The National Maritime Museum in London, England, supports this Web site, which explains the different types of galaxies.

Nemiroff, Robert, and Jerry Bonnell. "Astronomy Picture of the Day," NASA. Available online. URL: http://antwrp.gsfc.nasa.gov/apod/astropix.html. Accessed May 27, 2009. Amazing pictures of space, the Moon, and Earth are posted on this Web site every day.

O'Hanlon, Larry. "ABC News in Science: Space and Astronomy. Dark matter found in colliding galaxies," Australian Broadcasting Corporation, August 22, 2006. Available online. URL: http://www.abc.net.au/science/news/stories/2006/1720848. htm?space. Accessed May 29, 2009. O'Hanlon's article for ABC News in Science discusses the evidence for existence of dark matter.

Regents of the University of California. "What is a Galaxy?" 2001. Available online. URL: http://cse.ssl.berkeley.edu/SegwayEd/lessons/classifying_galaxies/student2. htm. Accessed May 29, 2009. On this Web site, different types of galaxies are described and pictures from the *Hubble Telescope* are provided as examples.

Space and Telescope Science Institute. "Newscenter," Hubblesite. Available online. URL: http://hubblesite.org/newscenter/archive/releases/category/. Accessed May 29, 2009. The Office of Public Outreach at the Space Telescope Science Institute (STScI) provides several pages of links related to the work of the *Hubble Telescope*.

Space.com. Available online. URL: http://www.space.com/scienceastronomy/. Accessed May 27, 2009. This Web site contains links to dozens of articles on topics related to astronomy.

Periodic Table of Elements

Legend:
```
 1   ← atomic number
 H   ← symbol
1.008 ← atomic weight
```

Numbers in parentheses are the atomic mass numbers of radioactive isotopes.

1	2	3	4	5	6	7	8	9	10	11	12	13	14	15	16	17	18
1 H 1.008																	2 He 4.003
3 Li 6.941	4 Be 9.012											5 B 10.81	6 C 12.01	7 N 14.01	8 O 16.00	9 F 19.00	10 Ne 20.18
11 Na 22.99	12 Mg 24.31											13 Al 26.98	14 Si 28.09	15 P 30.97	16 S 32.07	17 Cl 35.45	18 Ar 39.95
19 K 39.10	20 Ca 40.08	21 Sc 44.96	22 Ti 47.88	23 V 50.94	24 Cr 52.00	25 Mn 54.94	26 Fe 55.85	27 Co 58.93	28 Ni 58.69	29 Cu 63.55	30 Zn 65.39	31 Ga 69.72	32 Ge 72.59	33 As 74.92	34 Se 78.96	35 Br 79.90	36 Kr 83.80
37 Rb 85.47	38 Sr 87.62	39 Y 88.91	40 Zr 91.22	41 Nb 92.91	42 Mo 95.94	43 Tc (98)	44 Ru 101.1	45 Rh 102.9	46 Pd 106.4	47 Ag 107.9	48 Cd 112.4	49 In 114.8	50 Sn 118.7	51 Sb 121.8	52 Te 127.6	53 I 126.9	54 Xe 131.3
55 Cs 132.9	56 Ba 137.3	57-71*	72 Hf 178.5	73 Ta 180.9	74 W 183.9	75 Re 186.2	76 Os 190.2	77 Ir 192.2	78 Pt 195.1	79 Au 197.0	80 Hg 200.6	81 Tl 204.4	82 Pb 207.2	83 Bi 209.0	84 Po (210)	85 At (210)	86 Rn (222)
87 Fr (223)	88 Ra (226)	89-103‡	104 Rf (261)	105 Db (262)	106 Sg (263)	107 Bh (262)	108 Hs (265)	109 Mt (266)	110 Ds (271)	111 Rg (272)	112 Uub (285)		114 Uuq (285)		116 Uuh (292)		118 Uuo (?)

*lanthanide series:

57 La 138.9	58 Ce 140.1	59 Pr 140.9	60 Nd 144.2	61 Pm (145)	62 Sm 150.4	63 Eu 152.0	64 Gd 157.3	65 Tb 158.9	66 Dy 162.5	67 Ho 164.9	68 Er 167.3	69 Tm 168.9	70 Yb 173.0	71 Lu 175.0

‡actinide series:

89 Ac (227)	90 Th 232.0	91 Pa 231.0	92 U 238.0	93 Np (237)	94 Pu (244)	95 Am (243)	96 Cm (247)	97 Bk (247)	98 Cf (251)	99 Es (252)	100 Fm (257)	101 Md (258)	102 No (259)	103 Lr (260)

Index